# The
# Jack Schwager Trading Course

## Your complete guide to mastering the markets

## Reference Guide

**MARKETPLACE BOOKS**
GLENELG, MARYLAND

**Copyright © 2006 by Jack Schwager.**

**Cover Copyright © 2006 by Marketplace Books.**

**Published by Marketplace Books.**

**Reprinted by arrangement of Omega Research, Inc.**

**All rights reserved.**

Trade Station and Easy Language are registered trademarks of Omega Research, Inc.

Reproduction or translation of any part of this work beyond that permitted by section 107 or 108 of the 1976 United States Copyright Act without the permission of the copyright owner is unlawful. Requests for permission or further information should be addressed to the Permissions Department at Marketplace Books®.

Neither Jack Schwager nor Marketplace Books is advising anyone to trade or use any system illustrated in this video course. These are educational examples of the science of system testing and development that Mr. Schwager and Marketplace Books want to share with you. None of the information illustrated in these examples is to be construed as offers to buy or sell commodities, stocks, or any other financial instrument. None of the information presented purports to be a complete statement of all material facts related to trading.

Also, simulated performance results have certain inherent limitations; the results do not represent actual trading. Since the trades in this series have not been executed, the results may have under or over compensated for the impact, if any, of certain market factors, such as lack of liquidity. No representation is being made that the systems or ideas shown in this video course will produce the results that are described or illustrated.

This publication is designed to provide accurate and authoritative information in regard to the subject matter covered. It is sold with the understanding that neither the author nor the publisher is engaged in rendering legal, accounting, or other professional service. If legal advice or other expert assistance is required, the services of a competent professional person should be sought.

*From a Declaration of Principles jointly adopted by a Committee of the American Bar Association and a Committee of Publishers.*

ISBN–13: 978-1-59280-253-1
ISBN–10: 1-59280-253-2

Printed in the United States of America.

# Table of Contents

**Lesson 1:** Trading Systems: The key principals to success . . . . . . . . . . . . . . . . . . . . . . . .9

**Lesson 2:** Defining Your Trading System: Learn to Follow the Trends . . . . . . . . . . . .11

**Lesson 3:** Going Against The Trend: What does your personality say to you? . . . . . . .15

**Lesson 4:** Pattern Systems: Using technical analysis as a trading trigger . . . . . . . . . . .19

**Lesson 5:** Parameters: The building blocks of your trading system . . . . . . . . . . . . . .23

**Lesson 6:** Pitfalls: Systems are good but they're not guaranteed . . . . . . . . . . . . . . . . .27

**Lesson 7:** Choosing The Right Data For Your Stock Trading System . . . . . . . . . . . .35

**Lesson 8:** Choosing The Right Data For Your Futures Trading System. . . . . . . . . . .41

**Lesson 9:** Finalizing a System Concept: Diversifying Across Time and Markets . . . . .49

**Lesson 10:** Confirmation Conditions: Learn to fine-tune your trend
following systems . . . . . . . . . . . . . . . . . . . . . . . . . . . . . . . . . . . . . . . . . . . . . . . . . . . . . . .57

**Lesson 11:** Filters: Tight guarding your system to enhance your success . . . . . . . . . . .61

**Lesson 12:** When to Get Out: Key exit strategies for trend following systems. . . . . . .65

**Lesson 13, 14, 15, & 16:** Using Easy Language to Program and Test Your
Personal Trading Systems . . . . . . . . . . . . . . . . . . . . . . . . . . . . . . . . . . . . . . . . . . . . . . . . .73

**Lesson 17:** Using Chart Patterns as a Guide to Creating
Automated Trading Systems . . . . . . . . . . . . . . . . . . . . . . . . . . . . . . . . . . . . . . . . . . . . . 117

**Lesson 18 & 19:** How To Turn Your Own Idea Into a
Computerized Trading System . . . . . . . . . . . . . . . . . . . . . . . . . . . . . . . . . . . . . . . . . . . 131

**Lesson 20:** Optimization: Getting the most out of your trading system . . . . . . . . . . 177

**Lesson 21:** Just How Good Is It? The truth about simulated results . . . . . . . . . . . . . 181

**Lesson 22:** Quantifying Results: How to measure system performance . . . . . . . . . . 191

**Lesson 23 & 24:** Money Management: Translating your system results into cash. . . 203

Since writing three "Market Wizards" books based on my interviews with truly great traders, I have been besieged by inquiries from readers on virtually every aspect of trading. One of the most frequently asked questions has been, **"How do I find a Market Wizard that will take me under their wing and teach me to be a great trader?"**

The very question indicates a misguided belief that there is an easy path to riches. There is not. As the "Wizards" consistently confirm, trading success cannot be presented on a silver platter.

It is achieved *only* by a commitment to self-education and hard work. Every great trader I've encountered has been a dedicated student of the markets, developing and perfecting their own trading ideas and concepts along the way.

The knowledge I gained from the "Wizards," coupled with decades of personal trading, has provided me with more than enough content to formulate a comprehensive trading course teaching market enthusiasts how to design, test, and develop their *own* trading plan. The result is a complete "course" with 3 primary goals:

1. **Provide a Comprehensive Program:** I begin with the basics and progress through advanced topics, such as system programming and testing methodologies—all subjects essential for those seeking trading self-sufficiency.

2. **Meet Realistic Expectations:** I do not sugarcoat or shortcut the process. I cover all the steps required, and present a real-life perspective, providing hundreds of examples to show what happens when things work—as well as when they *don't* work. Moreover, examples are chosen based on their instructional value—<u>not</u> to make the system look good.

3. **Be Accessible to All:** The beginning trader will not find this course too complex, nor will the experienced player find it too basic. It covers the full range of the trading spectrum, with reference material every trader can, and should, come back to over time. In addition, no programming or mathematical knowledge is required.

I have tried to produce an honest product that provides the serious market student with the essentials for becoming a self-sufficient and successful trader. If you make the commitment of time and effort this course requires, I believe you will not only improve your performance in the markets, you'll save *years* of work learning the same material on your own, and probably save money by avoiding many of the key pitfalls! I hope this course helps you to create your own trading ideas and methods, much as the "Wizards" have done. Who knows, maybe you'll even become one of the traders I interview in my next "Market Wizards" work!

Sincerely,

Jack Schwager

# LESSON 1: WHY USE SYSTEMS AND AN OVERVIEW OF THIS SERIES

## WHAT THIS SERIES WILL AND WILL NOT TEACH YOU

**Subjects that will be covered:**

- How to design your own trading systems
- What data to use in testing systems
- How to test systems
- Major pitfalls to avoid
- Examples of trading systems
- Technical patterns that can be used as components of trading systems
- How to translate concepts into programming code—explained for nonprogrammers
- The importance of diversification
- How to optimize a system and whether optimization is valid
- Performance measures
- Portfolio construction
- Money management considerations

In short, this series will cover everything you need to know to construct your own trading methodology.

**What this series will not provide**

- A black box system that you blindly follow to make guaranteed profits

In short, you will have to do your own work, but this series will provide you with all the necessary tools.

## BENEFITS OF A MECHANICAL TRADING SYSTEM

**Six basic advantages of trading systems:**

1. Eliminates emotion
2. Eliminates need for constant decision making
3. Ensures consistency of approach
4. Risk Control

5. Same approach can be applied to many markets
6. Approach can be tested for statistical reliability

## STAND ALONE SYSTEMS VERSUS SYSTEMS AS TIMING TOOLS

Typically, it is assumed that systems are used to generate buy and sell signals that are automatically followed without any additional decision-making process. And, in most cases, this is indeed the preferred approach, as picking and choosing among trade signals will usually have a detrimental effect. However, in some instances, a trader may prefer to use systems as timing tools as opposed to an automated trading approach. Some possible reasons include:

1. The trader's personality may dictate against an automated approach.
2. The individual's intention may be investment not trading, with systems being used to time entry and exit from the investment.
3. The market may not lend itself to system trading (e.g., sustained bull market in stocks).

# LESSON 2: TRADING SYSTEMS DEFINED AND ILLUSTRATED — TREND-FOLLOWING SYSTEMS

A trading system is a set of rules that can be used to generate trade signals Trading systems can be classified in 3 general categories:

1. Trend-following
2. Counter-trend
3. Pattern

*Important Note: In this manual as well as in the video, we use daily prices for illustration. However, the price series (bars on chart) can be for any time length: monthly, weekly, 90-minute, 30-minute, etc.*

## THE BREAKOUT SYSTEM

The breakout is a simple but often very effective trend-following system. The system will provide a buy signal when the market closes higher than the highest high during the past "N" days and a sell signal when the market closes below the lowest low during the past "N" days. N is a *parameter* or *input* that has to be defined. **Figure** 2-1 shows the breakout system applied to the Deutsche mark for N = 80.

This system will tend to work very well during periods with long trends. However, the system will do poorly during periods of wide-swinging trading range markets (see **Figure** 2-2)

As an aside, the reason why most of the charts in this manual depict earlier years is that the computer simulation examples in this course were always applied to start dates of 1990 or earlier through 1997 or early 1998. Insofar as most of the system explanations begin with the starting period, most of the examples tend to be from earlier years. However, similar examples could also have been easily drawn from more recent years.

## TRADESTATION SYSTEM REPORT: PERFORMANCE SUMMARY

Some of the key performance statistics provided include:

**Total Net Profit**—Total dollar gain or loss.

**Average Trade**—The average profit (or loss) per trade.

**Maximum Drawdown**—The largest equity decline during the entire period.

**Profit factor**—Total dollars gained on winning trades divided by total dollars lost on losing trades.

**Return on Account**—Total Net Profit divided by the account size required (Maximum Drawdown + margin). This figure can be misleading if not properly understood. See next section.

**Figure** 2-3 provides an illustration of a typical Performance Summary table in TradeStation.

## UNDERSTANDING RETURN ON ACCOUNT

### Reasons Why Return on Account is Overstated

1. Most significantly, the indicated figure is for the entire test period (e.g., 8 years) as opposed to an annual average.

2. Available equity should be multiple of maximum drawdown (e.g., 5:1).

3. Future maximum drawdown should be assumed equal to two times past figures.

These factors imply an overstatement of 80:1!

8 x 5 x 2 = 80

**Figure** 2-1

12 *Jack Schwager's Complete Guide to Designing and Testing Trading Systems*

**Reasons Why Return on Account is Understated**

1. Drawdown from initial equity is usually much smaller than maximum drawdown and could even be zero.

2. Portfolio maximum drawdown will be much smaller than individual market maximum drawdown.

**Summary**

1. Although it is difficult to say how these factors net out, in order to lean on the conservative side, as a rough rule, one can divide stated percent returns by 2-3 times # of years—that is, for 8-year period divide by 16-24. Assuming a divisor of 20,

    **Example:** 160% return would imply 8% annual return

2. Remember for futures, system returns are **in addition to** interest rate returns, since margin funds collect interest.

3. True return figures must be equity-based not trade-based. Therefore, Performance Summary tables shown for systems provide only rough indications. Equity based performance analysis will be discussed later in this series.

## THE CROSSOVER MOVING AVERAGE SYSTEM

Moving averages provide a very simple means of smoothing a price series and making any trends more discernible. A simple moving average is defined as the average close of the past N days, ending in the current day. For example, a 10-day moving average would be equal to the average of the past 10 closes, including the current day. The term *moving average* refers to the fact that the set of numbers being averaged is continuously moving through time.

Typically moving averages are calculated using daily closes. However, moving averages could also be based on opens, highs, or an average of the open, high, low, and close. Also, moving averages can be calculated for time intervals of data other than daily.

The shorter the moving average, the more responsive it will be to price changes. A crossover moving average system uses two moving averages. A buy signal is generated when the shorter moving average crosses above the longer moving average; a sell signal is generated when the shorter moving average crosses below the longer moving average.

**Figure** 2-4 demonstrates how trading signals are generated in a crossover moving average system (using 3- and 10-day moving averages). The 3-day moving average column is calculated by taking the average of the past three closes ending with the indicated day. The 10-day column is analogous using ten closes. When the difference is positive (i.e., the 3-day moving average is greater than the 10-day moving average) the system is long, and when the difference is negative, the system is short. This system, similar to most systems we will illustrate, is always in the market. **Figure** 2-5 illustrates the application of a 10-day/50-day crossover moving average system to the same price chart illustrated in **Figure** 2-1.

## 80-DAY BREAKOUT STOCK EXAMPLE

For stocks, traders may prefer to trade a long only version of a trend-following system. There are two reasons for this:

1. Many traders will not short stocks, either because of the extra complications in going short or because they have a bias against short positions.
2. Historically, a bias against the short side of stocks can actually be justified by the strong secular uptrend in stocks—an uptrend that as will be seen later in this course does not have a counterpart in the futures markets.

A long only version of the breakout system would go long on an upside breakout signal and cover that position (i.e., move to neutral) on a downside breakout. **Figure** 2-6 compares the long-only version of the breakout with the standard version. **Figure** 2-7 shows that the performance table of the long-only version is identical to the performance table of the standard system segmented by long trades. The significance of this observation is that if a long-only version of a system is desired, it is not necessary to reprogram the system. The results can be obtained by checking the long trades only portion of the performance table for the standard version of the system.

# LESSON 3: TRADING SYSTEMS DEFINED AND ILLUSTRATED — COUNTER-TREND SYSTEMS

As the name implies, counter-trend systems generate signals opposite to the prevailing trend on the assumption that the trend has gone far enough and is prone to a reversal. Before explaining our examples of counter-trend systems, it is necessary to first define the terms of True Range and Average True Range.

## TRUE RANGE AND AVERAGE DAILY TRUE RANGE

The True Range is the daily range encompassing any gap from the previous day's (bar's) close. The True Range is more representative of the market's true volatility. For example, on a locked limit-up or limit-down day, the range would be equal to zero, but the True Range would equal the daily limit. The formula for the True Range is:

**True Range** = MaxList(H, C[1]) – MinList (L, C[1]), where

**MaxList**—A function that returns the highest value listed in parentheses. (Functions are fully explained later in this course.)

**MinList**—A function that returns the lowest value listed in parentheses.

**High** = Today's (current bar) high

**Low** = Today's (current bar) high

**C[1]** = Yesterday's (previous bar's) close

The True Range is illustrated in **Figure** 3-1.

The Average Daily True Range is the average True Range for the past N days, where N is a value that has to be specified.

## ADTR BAND COUNTER-TREND SYSTEM (VERSION 1)

This system generates two price bands, which are derived as follows:

**Upper Band**—N-day moving average + k * ADTR

**Lower Band**—N-day moving average - k * ADTR

N, and k are inputs that need to be defined (e.g., N=60, k=3) and ADTR stands for the N-day Average Daily True Range.

Buy and sell signals are generated by the following rules:

**Buy**—Reverse from short to long when the market closes below the lower band (i.e., when the market closes by more than k * ADTR below the N-day moving average).

**Sell**—Reverse from long to short when the market closes above the upper band (i.e., when the market closes by more than k * ADTR above the N-day moving average).

This system is illustrated in **Figures** 3-2 and 3-3. As can be seen in these charts, the system performs extremely well during choppy trading range markets, but is vulnerable to large, open-ended losses during sustained trends.

### ADTR BAND COUNTER-TREND SYSTEM WITH EXIT (VERSION 2)

This a variation of the previous system, with the one difference being that trades are exited at the median line (a line drawn midway between the two price bands, which is actually the moving average itself) rather than at the opposite band. In other words, this version has a less restrictive condition for exiting versus entering a trade. Therefore, in contrast to all the other systems examined thus far, this system will not always be in the market. **Figure** 3-4 illustrates this version of the ADTR Band Counter-trend system.

### ADTR BAND COUNTER-TREND SYSTEM WITH LIQUIDATION RULE (VERSION 3)

One problem with Version 1 of the ADTR Band Counter-trend system is that it can stay positioned on the wrong side of an extended trend. To limit the loss in this type of situation, this version of the system adds a liquidation rule. Specifically, the counter-trend position is liquidated if the market closes below a 125-day low (in the case of longs) or above the 125-day high (in the case of shorts). (Of course, the general form of this system allows for any value to be used, not just the 125-day value used in our illustration.) This version of the system is illustrated in **Figure** 3-5.

## ADTR BAND COUNTER-TREND SYSTEM WITH LIQUIDATION RULE & RE-ENTRY FILTER (VERSION 4)

One problem with Version 3 is that it is prone to repeated re-entries after the system is stopped out (see **Figure** 3-6). This version attempts to correct for this problem by filtering out signals that occur too soon after a same-direction trade has been liquidated. For example, a buy signal that occurs within 50 days of a long position being exited on the liquidation rule (i.e., a buy signal that occurs within 50 days of a 125-day low) is filtered out. (Of course, the general form of this system allows for any value to be used, not just the 50-day value used in our illustration.) **Figure** 3-7 illustrates this version of the system.

A comparison of the performance table for Version 4 versus Version 1 for the gold market shows a dramatic improvement in all the key performance measures (e.g., total net profit, return on account, profit factor). See **Figure** 3-8.

Next we apply the same systems to the stock Aluminum Company of America and compare Versions 1 and 4. In this case, however, the more elaborate Version 4 turns a profitable system into a near break-even system (See **Figure** 3-9). What is going on? In this case, most stop points witness little follow-through and only knock the system out of good trades (see **Figure** 3-10).

The foregoing example illustrates a number of important lessons:

1. Don't jump to conclusions based on a single market test.
2. What helps you in one case may—no will—hurt you in an another. The question is how the tradeoff will balance out.
3. More complex strategies are not necessarily better than simpler strategies.

So which form of the counter-trend system is better? The answer would depend on more complete testing. But that's not the point. The object here is to show how a counter-trend system works and to illustrate how a counter-trend system can be developed, not to promote any specific counter-trend system.

As a final word, it has been my experience that counter-trend systems usually have inferior performance to trend following systems. Therefore, these types of systems may be more useful for combining with trend-following systems as opposed to trading as stand-alone systems.

# LESSON 4: TRADING SYSTEMS DEFINED AND ILLUSTRATED — PATTERN SYSTEMS

Aren't trend and counter-trend systems also based on patterns? The answer, of course, is yes. The distinction here, however, is that the pattern used to generate trade signals is not dependent on the direction of prices prior to the occurrence of the pattern. Thus, the type of pattern used in this type of system could generate buy signals after an uptrend or downtrend, and the same would apply to sell signals.

## GAP SYSTEMS

An up gap is a day whose low is greater than the high of the previous day, leaving a gap on the chart. Similarly, a down gap is a day whose high is below the previous day's low.

The basic gap system reverses from long to short on a down gap day and reverses from short to long on an up gap day. **Figure** 4-1 shows a close-up of 1-day gap signals. Note that there are no signals on new gaps in the same direction as the current position. Although it is theoretically possible for this type of system to occasionally generate buy signals near lows and sell signals near highs and also be profitable during choppy, trading range periods (see **Figure** 4-2), it also witnesses periods of very poor performance. In fact, despite some excellent individual trades, on balance, the system loses money in the illustrated market.

Perhaps the problem is that 1-day gaps are too common. We change this system to require gaps to be multiday gaps. For example, **Figure** 4-3 illustrates this version of the system in which buy signals are generated by 5-day up gaps (i.e., today's low is greater than the high of the past 5 days) and sell signals by 5-day down gaps (i.e., today's high is lower than the low of the past 5 days).

The performance table for this version reflects a drastic reduction in trades and a major improvement in performance vis-à-vis the 1-day gap system. However, an examination of the trade-by-trade performance table shows a particularly large loss on an April 1993 buy signal. A check of the chart reveals that after generating a buy signal near a peak, this system stayed long for most of the ensuing downtrend (see **Figure** 4-4).

Looking at this chart, a vulnerability of our system becomes clear: The maximum loss on any individual trade is virtually unlimited because the pattern required to reverse the existing position may not occur, or at least not occur until an ensuing adverse trend has largely run its course. To correct for this problem, we incorporate a liquidation rule into our system: Exit short (long) if a close is greater (less) than the highest high (lowest low) during the N1-day period prior to the gap. A check of the performance table (for a value of N1=10) shows that this version of the system provided a significant improvement in profits and a smaller largest loss vis-à-vis the version without the liquidation rule.

## IMPORTANT GENERAL COMMENTS

What is the main point of the gap system discussion? If you answered "5-day gaps with a stop rule are better than 1-day gaps," you missed the point—even though this is probably true. Single examples don't prove anything. In our example, the 5-day gap system with a stop was better than the basic 1-day gap system, but this does not prove the point in general. Although this statement may be true, this hypothesis has to be tested over an entire portfolio and over a greater span of time.

Keep the following point in mind throughout this manual as well as the accompanying video series: You can't generalize the efficacy of a system from a single example and such inferences are not intended! The foregoing gap system discussion was intended to illustrate an example of a pattern type system and to demonstrate general techniques and concepts in developing system ideas and modifying systems based on observed signals.

## CONSECUTIVE CLOSE SYSTEMS

The basic version of the Consecutive Close system reverses to long following N consecutive up days (e.g., N=3) and reverses to short following N consecutive down days (see **Figure** 4-5). With N=3 the system generates a profusion of trades and exhibits generally poor performance.

In an effort to restrict signals to more significant situations, which presumably have a better chance for success, we require the day prior to the string of consecutive up days to be a 20-day low. Similarly, sell signals require N consecutive down days *and* a 20-day high prior to the string of consecutive down days. This modification can be thought of as a reversal condition because it assures that the string of consecutive closes reverses the prior trend. This version of the Consecutive Close system is illustrated in **Figure** 4-6, which depicts an instance in which 3 consecutive up closes provided a signal as well as an instance in which 3 consecutive down closes did not. The addition of the reversal condition greatly reduces the number of trade signals and transforms the system from a significant net loser to a moderate net winner.

Next we consider adding a liquidation rule to the system: Liquidate long on a close below the lowest low for the N-day (N=3) period beginning with the day before the first up day in the string (i.e., the 20-day low day). The liquidation rule for a short position would be analogous. The liquidation point is fixed at the time of the signal and does not change. In this case, the performance table shows that the addition of the liquidation rule actually hurts the results—a consequence of the whipsaws created by the liquidation rule outweighing the savings generated by restricting formerly open-ended losses. Does this mean the system is better without stops? Definitely not; again, one can't draw conclusions based on a single observation.

# LESSON 5: PARAMETERS AND PARAMETER SETS

## PARAMETER (SYSTEM INPUT)

A parameter is a *variable* constant. A parameter is a value that can be freely assigned in system in order to vary the timing of signals, but once assigned acts as a constant. For example, the number of past days whose high must be exceeded to generate a buy signal in a breakout system is a parameter. In TradeStation and other Omega products, *parameters* are called system *inputs*. The two terms refer to identical concepts and are totally interchangeable.

The same system with different parameters behaves very differently. **Figure 5-1** compares a breakout system with N=20 with a breakout system with N=100. Note that the signals generated by these two parameter values for the same system are quite different. Generally speaking, more sensitive parameter values (i.e., lower values in a breakout system) will provide more timely valid signals (**Figure** 5-1) at the expense of generating more false signals (**Figure** 5-2).

## PARAMETER SET (INPUT COMBINATION)

Most systems contain more than one parameter. A parameter set is a specific set of values for all the parameters in a system. For example, the values for the two moving averages in a crossover moving average system constitute a parameter set. The same system with different parameter sets can behave very differently. **Figure 5-3** contrasts the signals generated by a crossover moving average system with a parameter set of 5/20 versus the same system with a parameter set of 15/150. As was the case in the breakout system illustration, the more sensitive version of the system (5/20) provides more timely entries, but at the expense of more false signals.

Although less sensitive parameter sets are more difficult to trade, because they get into trades later and give up more profits before a reversal signal is received, in my experience, they are generally much more profitable. However, don't take my word for it; do your own testing.

## PARAMETER SET LIST

A parameter set list is a list of all the parameter sets that will be tested for a given system. **Figure** 5-4 provides an illustration of a parameter set list for a crossover moving average system with three parameters: a short-term moving average, a long-term moving average, and a time delay. The time delay is a parameter that represents the number of days one waits after a signal to confirm that the signal is still intact. For example, if the short-term moving average crosses above the long-term moving average and the time delay = 5, five days after the crossover, the system would reverse from short to long if the short-term moving average was still above the long-term moving average. If it were not, the prior crossover would be considered a false signal and ignored. The time delay parameter is an example of a confirmation condition, a trend-following system modification discussed in detail in Lesson 10.

The list in **Figure** 5-4 contains 60 parameter sets. Note that each parameter is increased in jumps (e.g., increments of 10 for the short-term moving average). As will be discussed in the next section, it is highly inefficient (if not impossible) to test every possible combination of parameter set values. Also, such intensive testing is totally unnecessary, as it provides little, if any, additional useful information versus a sparse parameter set list, such as the one illustrated in **Figure** 5-4.

## PARAMETER MULTIPLICITY

Parameter sets can multiply like rabbits. For example, a system with 3 parameters and 10 tested values for each parameter would yield a parameter set list with 1,000 parameter sets. If there were 6 parameters with 10 tested values, there would 1,000,000 parameter sets. Obviously, there is a need to limit the number of parameters and the number of values tested for each parameter. For example, if the system illustrated in **Figure** 5-4 were tested for every possible combination of parameter values within the ranges indicated in this illustration (short-term moving average: 1-60, long-term moving average: 2-120, and time delay: 1-15), there would be a total of 80,550 combinations (avoiding duplications). **Figure** 5-4 adequately tests this same parameter set region with only 60 parameter sets.

Besides the impracticability of testing all, or even a significant portion of all parameter sets, such a detailed test would not provide any meaningful additional information. For example, if a 20/85 moving average combination did better than a 20/80 moving average combination (for the same time delay parameter), there would be no reason to believe that this difference represented anything more than chance variation. In other words, there would be no reason to assume that the 20/85 combination would do better in the future. In fact, as we will see later in this course, it is even questionable whether performance differences between significantly different parameter values are predictive of future performance rankings. Therefore, there is no need to test small increments in parameter values.

Also note that we can always do a new test run including other parameter sets if the best performing parameter set includes a parameter with a value at the extreme of the tested range. For example, if a time delay of 5 (the lowest value tested in **Figure** 5-4) appears to be the best value, we can do another test run using lower time delay values.

## FOUR TYPES OF PARAMETERS (SYSTEM INPUTS)

Conceptually, it might be useful to define four types of parameters:

1. **Continuous**—A continuous parameter can take on any value within a given range. A percentage price penetration would be an example of a continuous parameter. By definition, a continuous parameter can assume an infinite number of values. For example, a percentage price penetration could be set to 1.0 or 1.1 or any value in between.

2. **Discrete**—A discrete parameter can only assume integer values. For example, the parameter representing the number of days in a breakout system can be equal to 80 or 81, but not any number in between.

3. **Code**—A code parameter is used to represent a definitional classification. Thus, there is no significance to the cardinal value of a code parameter. As an example of a code parameter, assume we wish to test a simple breakout system using three different definitions of a breakout (buy case): 1) *close* above previous N-day *high*; 2) *high* above previous N-day *high*; and 3) *close* above previous N-day *high close*. We could test each of these systems separately, but it might be more efficient to use a parameter to specify the intended classification. Thus, a parameter value of 0 might indicate the first definition, a value of 1 the second definition, and a value of 2 the third definition. Note that there are only three possible values for this parameter and that there is no significance to incremental changes in parameter values.

4. **Fixed or Nonoptimized**—Normally, a parameter (of any type) will be allowed to assume different values in testing a system. However, in systems with a large number of parameters, it may be necessary to fix some parameter values in order to avoid an excessive number of parameter sets. Such parameters are called *nonoptimized parameters*. For example, a system might include a backup stop rule that only rarely comes into play. Any parameters used to define the stop rule could be fixed, since variation in these parameter values would not greatly impact the results.

Why then define such values as parameters instead of constants? Because, doing so gives us much greater flexibility. For example, after initial testing, we may decide we wish to change the value of a parameter previously assumed to be fixed. By defining this parameter at the outset as a parameter, as opposed to a constant, we avoid having to alter the system code in such a situation.

# LESSON 6: PITFALLS!

In this lesson we will be discussing the major pitfalls related to system trading. An awareness and understanding of these pitfalls may well be the single most important subject matter discussed in this series.

**THE WELL CHOSEN EXAMPLE**

**Figures** 6-1 and 6-2 illustrate an actual system. As can be seen, this system seems to generate incredible trade signals, repeatedly going long near bottoms and reversing to short near tops. Based on these illustrations, you might be quite tempted to trade this system, and perhaps even to spend hundreds or thousands of dollars to learn the "secret" of this apparently great system.

What are the rules of this incredible system? Quite simply this: Reverse from long to short whenever today's close is greater than the highest high during the past 90 days and reverse from short to long whenever today's close is less than the lowest low during the past 90 days. That's all there is to it. But before you rush out to trade this system, examine **Figures** 6-3, 6-4, 6-5 and 6-6, which illustrate the identical system applied to another market—coffee. In this case, although the system witnesses some periods of profitable trades, these gains are totally overwhelmed by several giant losses. In fact, for the period depicted in **Figures** 6-3 to 6-6, this system lost over $73,000 per contract!

The mock offer on the video for the SRD (Super Razzle Dazzle) system was intended to bring home three critical points, which we label "cardinal rules."

> CARDINAL RULE 1: Any, repeat any, system can be made to look great using a few well-chosen examples.

In fact, I believe it is virtually impossible to devise a system that can't be made to look great on some segment of market price history. Therefore...

> CARDINAL RULE 2: Never, repeat never judge a system based on a few examples.

And finally,

> CARDINAL RULE 3: What works in one case may kill you in the next.

The intended message of the foregoing discussion is not merely that one needs to be on guard against well-chosen system examples in articles, advertisements and direct mail. You also need to be wary of well-chosen examples in your own system testing. Don't jump to conclusions based on a few test cases—they may simply be well chosen examples by chance. Always do sufficient testing.

As a tangential comment, the subject of well-chosen examples also has implications for single market systems versus multimarket systems. The argument for developing individual systems for each market, or at least selecting specific parameter sets for each market, is that each market may have its own individual characteristics, and therefore such customization could theoretically yield more effective systems. The argument against such an approach (vis-à-vis using the same system and parameter sets for a broad group of markets) is that it is far more prone to the well-chosen example pitfall. As a related point, it is also far more difficult to reliably test systems that have been customized market by market.

## UNREALISTIC ASSUMPTIONS

### Understating Transaction Costs

The failure to adequately account for transaction costs can distort system test results. It should be emphasized that transaction costs are not merely commission costs but also include *slippage*, which can often be greater than the commission costs. *Slippage* is the difference between the assumed fill (e.g., midpoint between bid and asked prices, midpoint of opening or closing ranges, stop point) and the actual fill. Because market orders will be filled at the asked prices for buys and the bid prices for sells, actual fills will tend to be worse than the midpoint between bid and asked prices or the midpoint in the opening and closing ranges. Slippage can be particularly large for systems using stop orders, since stop orders can be filled well beyond the stop price. Therefore, realistic transaction costs are especially critical for systems using stops.

To illustrate the distortion that can arise if transaction costs are not incorporated (or adequately accounted for) in test results, we compare results for the Close Comparison System (also commonly referred to as a momentum system) using two different parameter values. This system will reverse from long to short when the close is less than the close of N days ago and reverse from short to long when the close is greater than the close of N days ago. **Figure** 6-7 illustrate the Close Comparison System for N=10.
**Figure** 6-8 compares the results of this system for two different values of N: 10 and 180 *without incorporating transaction costs*. This comparison seems to suggest that

the value N=10 does significantly better than the value N=180, generating nearly double the net profits. **Figure** 6-9 makes the same comparison, but this time incorporating a more realistic transaction cost of $50 per contract. The results of this comparison are dramatically different. Once transaction costs are included, the system using a parameter value of 10 is transformed into a net losing system, while the system with a parameter value of 180 is still profitable.

The reason for this drastic change in results is that the system using a parameter value of 10 is extremely active, generating numerous trades. Failing to include transaction costs will therefore greatly overstate the system's true performance. This example illustrates that failing to include transaction costs (or adequately account for such costs) can lead to misleading results and totally erroneous system comparisons.

**Unrealistic Entry Assumptions**

Occasionally, trade execution will not be possible because the market is locked at the daily permissible limit. If one assumes execution in such a situation, simulated results may dramatically overstate actual performance. **Figure** 6-10 illustrates a breakout system that signals a buy in the early part of a string of limit-up days. Realistically, this buy order would probably not be filled until the market traded freely, denoted on the chart with the label "Actual Buy." In similar fashion, albeit to a much more limited extent, the actual sell price proved to be worse than the signal sell price. As a result of these disparities, this trade, which based on the signal prices seemed to be extremely profitable ($15,900 per contract), was actually a net loser (-$6,075 per contract) if realistic entry assumptions were used.

Another more common entry assumption error some traders make in system testing is to assume entry on the close of the signal day, even though the information for the signal is not actually available until the close. Such a trading simulation will be distorted because it will yield results that could not have been obtained in the real world. If trading signals cannot be generated until after the close, then execution must be assumed to occur on the next day.

**KITCHEN SINK APPROACH—PARAMETER OVERKILL**

This error involves throwing a multitude of parameters into a system. The embellished breakout system described on the video includes 360,000,000 parameter set combinations even though no single parameter set is tested for more than 10 values. In systems of this type, with sufficient computer testing, one can always find some parameter set combination that did great in the past. The more parameter sets included, the greater the danger the system will be overfit to past data, and the less likely the system will continue to exhibit superior performance in the future.

## TRADING RESULTS REFLECT MARKET NOT SYSTEM

Typically, traders will attribute the results of a system entirely to the system itself. However, very often, the performance results of a system have more to do with the market being tested than the system. For example, consider the extreme low bar in **Figure** 6-11. Virtually all systems would have been short this market (short sterling) at this point. The extreme loss that would have been witnessed by such systems on the following day was far more a consequence of the market, which moved from a contract low to a near one-year high in the space of one day, than the result of any inherent flaw in the system. It is hard to conceive how any trend-following system could have avoided this loss.

**Figure** 6-12 reflects the reverse case. In this instance, the illustrated market (Japanese yen) witnessed a protracted, nearly uninterrupted price slide. The fact that a trend-following system was very profitable in this market during the period depicted would tell you very little about the efficacy of the system, since virtually any trend-following system would have done extremely well in this market. Once again, the results tell you more about the market than the system.

One way to check whether the performance of a system is due to inherent attributes or is simply a consequence of the markets tested is to compare the results with the results of a generic system (e.g., basic breakout or crossover moving average), tested for the same markets over the same time period. If the tested system is superior to a generic system, then it may well have intrinsic merit. If it is not, one can assume that the favorable performance was a consequence of the markets tested, not the result of any special merit of the system tested.

## APPLES AND ORANGES PITFALL—SYSTEM COMPARISONS MUST MATCH

For a comparison of two systems to be valid, the simulations should match in each of the following three factors:

1. **Transaction costs**—This point has already been discussed.

2. **Markets**—The two simulations should be based on identical market portfolios. If the two portfolios are not precisely matching (even if they have the majority of markets in common), a comparison of the system results does not say anything about the relative merit of each system. To simplify the illustration of this point, we will assume each portfolio consists of only one market—the same conclusions, however, would apply equally to more realistic multimarket portfolios.

**Figure** 6-13 compares the performance of System X and System Y (actually both are crossover moving average systems using different parameter values) run on two different markets. Based on this comparison, one might conclude that System X is far better. **Figure** 6-14 compares the same two systems, but this time run on the same market: the Japanese yen. Now, it is evident that System Y is substantially superior. Similarly, **Figure** 6-15 compares the same two systems, running both on the other market in the original comparison: heating oil. Once again, it is clear that System Y is far superior. In fact, in this instance, System X is a significant net loser. Thus, it is obvious that System Y is far superior to System X if each system is compared in the same market, the exact opposite conclusion implied by a comparison of the two systems across different markets.

Although few traders would make the mistake of comparing two systems each run on a different market, the implications of this simple example would apply equally to comparisons of similar, but nonmatching, portfolios. In other words, the same distortion can occur if systems are compared across any nonmatching portfolios (even if they have many markets in common)

3. **Time Period**—System comparisons must be based on identical time periods. Even small differences in test periods can make large differences in performance results. For example, **Figure** 6-16 illustrates the performance of a breakout system with N=30 applied to the gold market for the period 1/1/79 through 3/20/98. As can be seen, the system realizes a net profit of $2670.00 and an average profit per trade of $330.25.

*(Note: the corresponding figures mentioned on the tape—$15,000 and $190, respectively—are wrong because the start date on the screen at the time of taping was inadvertently set to 10/1/79 instead of 1/1/79. Therefore, the performance contrast between this start date and a one-year later start date is even substantially greater than implied on the tape.)*

However, as can be seen in **Figure** 6-17, if the start of the test period began only one year later, the entire profit of the system would disappear.

Why such a large discrepancy between two start dates only one year apart? **Figure** 6-18 provides the explanation. As can be seen in this chart, the system generated an extraordinarily profitable buy signal in 1979, capturing the entire subsequent historic bull move before surrendering part of the profits in early 1980. This one trade accounted for the total profit realized by the system during the entire 1979-early 1998 period. Therefore, a simulation beginning only one year later shows drastically different results.

The foregoing example is intended to emphasize the importance of exactly matching test dates in system comparisons. Therefore, if you test a system, and one year later you want to compare the performance of this system to a new system that you have developed, either match the current system test dates to the old system, or retest the old system to match current test dates. However, what you should not do is test the new system through the current date and compare it with the old system, which was tested through an earlier test date.

## HINDSIGHT

Perhaps the most serious (and probably the most common) error made in testing trading systems is allowing hindsight to affect the test results. "Hindsight" refers to using information that would not have been known during the period used to test the system. Using hindsight can grossly overstate the true performance potential of a system. There are four key ways that hindsight can enter into system results:

1. **Selecting Markets**—You test a system on a list of markets and then use only the results for the markets that performed well. This is a form of hindsight, because one can't define the markets that did well until after the fact. It is important to distinguish between trading and evaluation. It is perfectly fine to decide to *trade* only markets that performed well in the past; the point here is that the system *evaluation* should be based on all the markets tested, not just those that did well.

2. **Selecting Time Period**—You test a system over several length time periods, going from longer to shorter or vice versa, and assume the best period is most representative of the system's performance. Actually, all the periods tested should be considered as part of the evaluation process.

3. **Selecting Parameter Sets**—You test a system for a parameter set list and then base the system evaluation on the best performing parameter set. Once again, since there is no way of knowing which would be the best performing parameter set before the fact, results that use this information are highly biased. Here too, it is necessary to distinguish between trading and evaluation. It is perfectly fine to decide to *trade* the parameter set that performed best in the past; the point here is that the *evaluation* of the system should be based on all the parameter sets tested, not just the one that did best.

**Figure** 6-19 illustrates the equity chart for a three-market portfolio (Japanese yen, T-bond, and S&P500) using a simple breakout system, tested for values N=10 to N=150, and basing trade signals on the best performing parameter value for each market. (To approximately balance the portfolio in terms of market volatility, it is assumed that the position size in the T-bond and Japanese yen markets is five contracts and the position size in the S&P500 market is one contract.) Note the incredible performance that results from this approach. The catch, however, is that we would not have known the best performing parameter set in each market until after the fact. The stellar performance reflected in **Figure** 6-19 was achieved by using hindsight in a system with only one parameter set. Imagine the performance that could be achieved by using hindsight in a system with multiple parameter sets. Such performance results, however, would be highly biased and totally unrepresentative of the system's true potential.

4. **Modifying System to Mitigate Past Bad Events**—Imagine we test a system and find it gives the false signal illustrated in **Figure** 6-20. Upon closer examination, we notice that the buy signal in question was the fifth consecutive up close (see **Figure** 6-21). We then create an additional rule to the system, stipulating that buy signals that occur after five or more consecutive up closes are not taken. This rule will eliminate the false signal in question. However, this rule makes no theoretical sense and is simply a consequence of our hindsight examination of trading signals. Evaluating the system performance after such changes have been made would yield distorted results. Also, this type of artificial system modification could easily hurt performance in other markets (or even the same market during another time period).

The foregoing is not intended to imply that there is anything wrong with examining system signals for ideas as to how a system should be modified. On the contrary, such an examination is an important step in the system development process. However, the distinction here is the difference between modifying a system to fix oversights or errors versus modifying a system to improve specific past events. Filtering a buy signal that occurs after 5 up closes makes no logical sense and is just a matter of using hindsight to create a rule that fits the past data. In contrast, noticing that a system can sometimes allow an open-ended loss, and then changing the system rules to avert such a possibility is an example of a logic-based rule change. If a rule change makes sense, it should help performance in other markets on balance. To keep such valid rule changes from muddying the results because of hindsight, we can use the data from one market to fine tune the system rules and then test the system on other markets.

To avoid the hindsight pitfall, define the following *before* testing:
- Markets in portfolio (as well as the position size for trades)
- Time period for test
- Parameter set list

As will be explained in Lesson 21, the average of all parameter sets tested (assuming this list is defined before testing) represents a reasonable measure of performance. Again, these comments pertain to testing and system evaluation. For actual trading, one may well want to trade only a portion of the markets tested. Also, by definition, to generate trading signals, it is necessary to select specific parameter sets. However, the performance of hindsight selected parameter sets applied to a hindsight selected subset of markets should not be used to *evaluate* the system. This very critical topic will be revisited in greater detail in Lesson 21.

As a final word, when evaluating a system, always ask yourself the following question: Do the performance results depend in any way on information that would not have been known during the time of the test period? If the answer is yes, the results are suspect.

# LESSON 7: DATA—STOCK TRADERS ONLY

*Important Note: This lesson is only pertinent to traders who are interested in applying trading systems to stock data. Futures only traders can skip to the next lesson.*

## A CRITICAL AND COMMONPLACE BLUNDER

Most people testing trading systems on stock data commit an enormous error. Whenever a system is tested, the standard implicit assumption is that each trade is for the same size (e.g., 1, 100 shares). Imagine testing a system on a portfolio of stocks ranging in price from $2 to $100. Would it be reasonable to test the system using an assumption of equal trade size (e.g., 100 shares) in all markets? **Figure** 7-1 illustrates the consequences of trading two disparately priced stocks ($2 and $100) in the same position size. As can be seen in the top table, an equal dollar price change in each stock would have an equal impact on profit/loss, but represent a 50% change in the low-priced stock and only a 1% price change in the high-priced stock. The lower table shows that an equal percent price change in each stock would have 50 times the dollar impact in the high-priced stock as in the low-priced stock. Obviously, it makes no sense to trade stocks priced at widely disparate levels in the same position size.

The same mistake occurs when testing an individual stock because of the huge ratio of the highest high to the lowest low in the data range. For example, a $1 move in Chrysler when the stock is $1 represents a 100% price change, while a $1 move when the stock is at $40 represents only a 2.5% price change. It doesn't make any sense for these two events to have the same impact on the system's profit/loss. Before explaining how position size can be adjusted to compensate for widely varying stock price levels, it is first necessary to explain how and why stock prices are adjusted for stock splits.

## SPLIT ADJUSTED STOCK PRICES

Historical price data is adjusted for stock splits and will not reflect the price the stock actually traded at the time (assuming that there have been one or more splits). Adjusting historical prices for intervening stock splits is necessary to avoid distortions. For example, if a stock trading at $50 splits 2:1, all prices prior to the split must be halved, otherwise the price series will show the price declining from $50 to $25 on the day of the split (assuming the stock is unchanged that day). To avoid such distortions, stock price data is split adjusted. Therefore, if a stock witnessed three 2:1 splits it would imply that a $1 change for the early part of the data was actually an $8 per share change at the time.

## ADJUSTING POSITION SIZE TO COMPENSATE FOR WIDELY VARYING PRICE LEVELS

Instead of assuming that each trade signal is always transacted for the same number of shares, it makes much more sense to assume that each trade is for an equal dollar amount—for example, $1,000. Then for each signal, the number of shares traded would be given by the following formula:

*Number of shares = $1000/ price*

For example, if price = $50, the number of shares = 20. This approach will have the desirable consequence that equal percent price changes will have equal profit/loss effects (see **Figure** 7-2).

How do we calculate the number of shares for past trades when we have only split adjusted price data and not the actual prices traded in the past? Fortunately, as it turns out, adjusted price data can be substituted for actual price data in the above formula for the number of shares. A detailed explanation is provided in **Figure** 7-3

# HOW TO DETERMINE NUMBER OF SHARES IN TRADE

**Definitions**

> **Adjusted Price**—Prices adjusted for stock splits. This is conventional form of price data.
>
> **Actual Price**—The actual price of a stock at each past point of time.
>
> Adjusted Price = Actual Price/Cumulative Split Ratio
>
> **Example:** Actual Price = $20 and subsequently two 2:1 splits
>
> Adjusted Price = $20/4 = $5

**Why Adjusted Prices and Actual Price Yield Same Results**

> To Determine # of Shares at any past time so that position value = $1,000:
>
> # Shares = $1,000/Actual Price

The P/L of this position would be equal to:

$$\text{\# Shares} * \text{Actual Price Change}$$
$$\text{Or}$$
$$(\$1{,}000/\text{Actual Price}) * \text{Actual Price Change}$$

We have adjusted prices, not actual prices. Note that if we use the adjusted price instead of the actual price, the # of shares would be overstated by the cumulative split ratio, but the price change would be understated by the same ratio. Therefore in the P/L equation, these two effects would cancel each other out.

**Determining Number of Shares Using Adjusted Price**

To determine # of Shares at any past time so that position value = $1,000:

$$\text{\# Shares} = \$1{,}000/\text{Adjusted Price}$$

The P/L of this position would be equal to:

$$(\$1{,}000/\text{Adjusted Price}) * \text{Adjusted Price Change}$$

**Example:**

*Assumptions:*
Two 2:1 splits; cumulative split ratio = 4:1
Current Price = $40
Old Actual Price = $20
Old Adjusted Price = $5
Constant investment size = $1000

*Actual old price goes up from $20 to $ 24 (20% increase)*
# actual shares = $1000/$20 = 50
and Total P/L = 50 * $4 = $200

*Using adjusted formula:*
# shares = $1000/$5 = 200
and Total P/L = 200 * $1 = $200

*Assuming same 20% increase for current price:*
# shares = $1000/$40 = 25
and Total P/L = 25 * $8 = $200

Of course, the position size assumption doesn't have to be equal dollar. The equal dollar position size assumption, however, is far more likely to be representative of actual trading than the conventional equal share size assumption. The key general principal is:

> CARDINAL RULE 4: Test systems in a way that reflects the way they will actually be traded.

The standard implicit assumption of a constant trade size on split-adjusted data (e.g., 1, 100 shares) violates this rule.

To illustrate the type of distortion that can arise by naively using a constant share size assumption to test a system, **Figure** 7-4 compares the performance of a 12/120 crossover moving average system applied to Wal Mart for two position size assumptions: constant single contract versus constant $1,000. As can be seen, the percent return is more than 7 times greater trading $1,000 on each signal.

To explain the extreme disparity in these results for the exact same system applied to the same market, **Figure** 7-5 depicts the equity curves (lower graphs in each chart) for each of the two position size assumptions. Note that the March 1982 buy, which captured a 258% price gain between entry and exit (yielding an equivalent percent return for the constant dollar investment) only accounted for a $1.74 gain per share. The impact of this per share gain on total return would have been totally swamped by the gains and losses on more recent trades when the price of the stock was far higher.

The problem is that the conventional approach tends to drastically underweight trades in earlier years versus recent years (or more generally, low-priced years versus high-priced years), especially in stocks that have witnessed large price gains and multiple splits. Therefore, even huge percentage gain trades in early years, such as the one illustrated in **Figure** 7-5, will only marginally affect the total profit/loss. Conversely, the constant share size assumption will hugely overstate the impact of trades in later, higher-priced years. For example, the one trade highlighted in **Figure** 7-6 accounted for over 60% of total profits for the entire period in the constant share trade size case, but only 10% of total profits in the constant dollar trade size case.

## STOCK BUY-AND-HOLD COMPARISONS

To evaluate whether favorable performance statistics are in part due to the system being tested or are strictly a consequence of price appreciation in the stock, it is useful to compare the system results with buy-and-hold results. However, it should be emphasized that system results based on a constant dollar trade size (e.g., $1,000) cannot be directly compared to buy-and-hold results for the same number of starting shares. For example, if price starts at $5 and goes to $50, 200 shares, which equal $1,000 at the start, would equal $10,000 at the end. Meanwhile the system results continue to assume a $1,000 trade size on each signal. Therefore, the buy-and-hold case is implicitly assuming a much larger average position size.

There are two possible adjustment methods that can be used to allow valid comparisons between system and buy-and-hold results:

1. Compound the system number of contracts per trade by the ratio of current equity/$1,000. In this approach, a second factor is added to calculate the number of shares: the ratio of current equity to the assumed starting equity. If the starting equity = $1,000, then this ratio is equal to *($1000 + Net Profit)/$1000*. Therefore, the number of shares is given by the formula:

    *Number of shares = ($1000/price) * ($1000 + Net Profit)/$1000.*

    Thus, if the system has made $2000, the second factor in the equation would equal 3, because there is now $3000 available instead of $1000.

    Note that this approach breaks down if the loss exceeds $1000, since it would result in a negative equity ratio, which in turn would imply a negative number of shares—a nonsensical result.

    It should be pointed out that the *maximum intraday drawdown* and the *return on account* statistics in the TradeStation P/L table should **never** be used for a buy-and-hold approach. Reason: Since by definition there is only one trade in the buy-and-hold case (a buy at the start of the data stream), the maximum drawdown will be the largest dip relative to that starting point (drawdown in TradeStation is measured only relative to trade entry), even if there are much larger drawdowns later in the equity stream. Therefore, the maximum intraday drawdown will usually be substantially understated, and by implication, the return on account (which is equal to total net profit divided by the maximum intraday drawdown, assuming margin requirements are ignored) will be equivalently overstated. Therefore percent return comparisons with the buy-and-hold case should use a compounded percent return statistic, which is given by the following formula (and not the return on account statistic in the P/L table):

*Compounded Percent Return = 100 \* (Net Profit/1000)*

2. Adjust the number of shares in the buy-and-hold position to the same number of contracts traded by the system ($1,000/price) each time the system has a trade signal. **Figure** 7-7 illustrates this second approach. Note that the buy-and-hold approach (lower chart) is always long, but that the position size is adjusted at each system signal to equal the system position size ($1,000/price).

## DIVIDENDS

The absence of dividends in system performance calculations is a source of distortion. Specifically, when long, dividend profits are not included, and when short, dividend obligations are not deducted. Ideally, dividend additions or subtractions should be included in profit/loss calculations. However, the correction is sufficiently onerous and the distortion sufficiently small so that this adjustment can generally be ignored by most traders.

# LESSON 8: DATA—FUTURES TRADERS ONLY

## TRADE SIZE ADJUSTMENTS IN THE CASE OF FUTURES

For futures, the problem of varying price levels is far less severe because, contrary to common perceptions of futures prices being more volatile than stock prices, the range between high and low prices tends to be far more moderate in futures than in stocks. This is true because of the huge secular uptrend in stocks, which has no counterpart in futures. See, for example, **Figures** 8-1, 8-2, and 8-3, which depict monthly prices for three sample stocks: American Express (an average performing high cap stock), General Motors (a below-average performing high cap stock), and Disney (an above-average performing high cap stock). The high-to-low price ratios in these stocks range from 5:1 to 120:1 and all reflect a pronounced uptrend over time. These characteristics provide a representative sample for stocks in general.

In contrast, **Figures** 8-4, 8-5, and 8-6 depict monthly prices for three futures markets: crude oil, soybeans, and the Swiss franc. Note that the high-to-low price ratios in these markets tend to be much lower: approximately 2:1 to 4:1. (Although some futures markets exhibit moderately higher ratios, the sample selected is fairly representative.) Also note that there is no dominant tendency for prices to trend higher over time; rather futures markets tend to move in broad ranges. Therefore, in the case of futures, the typical range of position size, whether based on price (or contract value, which is equivalent) or some volatility measure (e.g., margin), will be much smaller (typically, 2-4:1 instead of an average of 20:1 or more). Although this implies that the distortion due to assuming a constant contract/share price will be much more muted in the case of futures (vis-à-vis stocks), in order for the TradeStation performance table to be more representative, it is probably still preferable to use one of the following adjustments (for non-interest rate markets):

### Method 1—Using Contract Value

Divide some multiple of equity by contract value:

$$\text{\# Contracts} = K * Equity/Contract\ Value \quad (e.g., K=4)$$

**Example:** Equity = $100,000, Wheat = $4.00, 5,000 bushels per contract, K=4

$$\text{\# Contracts} = (\$400,000/\$20,000) = 20$$

### Method 2—Using Margin

Divide equity by a multiple of margin:

$$\# Contracts = Equity/ K * Margin \quad (e.g., K=5)$$

**Example:** Equity = $100,000, Margin=$2000, K=5

$$\# Contracts = (\$100,000/\$10,000) = 10$$

### Method 3—Using Volatility

Adjust trade size using some measure of volatility, trading fewer contracts when volatility is higher

### ACTUAL SERIES

In contrast to stocks where there is only one price series for each market (i.e., each stock), in the case of futures, contracts trade for only a limited duration. Therefore, computer testing of systems, which at the absolute minimum should span at least 5-10 years, implies using price data for many contracts. At first glance, it might seem that a system should be tested on a succession of contracts with the results combined at the end. However, the use of actual price data presents three major problems:

**Problem 1:** Such an approach would be quite cumbersome because of the large number of individual tests implied for each market. For example, a 15- year test of a market with 6 contracts per year would imply testing the system on 90 separate series and then somehow combining the results. All this for a test of just one market!

**Problem 2:** It is entirely possible that the system status (long, short, or neutral) may be different in the contract one is switching out of versus the contract one is switching into. For example, the time has come to switch from July soybeans to November soybeans and the system is short in July, but long in November. Do you switch from short to long even though there has not been a buy signal, or do you liquidate the July position and wait for a new signal in November, or do you follow some other course of action?

**Problem 3:** This is by far the most serious problem. For many markets, there is simply not enough liquid data available to initialize the system for the new contract at the time of rollover. In many futures markets, contracts only become liquid about 5-9 months before expiration, which implies only about 2-6 months of useable past data at the time of rollover. For example, **Figure** 8-7 illustrates that at the approximate time of rollover from the March to June Japanese yen contract, there were only about 4 months of past price data available during which the new contract had been relatively liquid. (A prevalence of one-tick or very narrow price ranges implies the contract was traded very inactively during the given period.) **Figure** 8-8 illustrates that at the approximate time of rollover from the March to June Italian bond contract (an actively traded foreign bond contract); there were only about 2 months of useable past price data available. By definition, most long-term systems need more than 2-4 months of data to establish a signal. Therefore actual price series may not merely be cumbersome to use (Problem 1), but impossible to use.

## NEAREST FUTURES

The foregoing section made it clear that using actual contract data is often not a viable solution in system testing. There is an obvious need to link futures contracts together to form a single price series for each market. The most common method of linking futures contracts is the *nearest futures* approach. This method uses the nearest futures contract for the price series until a specific rollover date, typically the contract's expiration date, and then begins using the next contract for the date series, and so on.

Nearest futures are commonly used to depict multiyear price charts and accurately reflect past price levels. However, nearest futures are totally unusable for testing systems because of price gaps that commonly exist between old and new contracts at the time of rollover. For example, consider the enormous price gap in the cotton chart depicted in **Figure** 8-9. This price gap is indistinguishable from an enormous price collapse. However, in actuality all that occurred was a switch from one contract to another contract (in this case, from an old crop contract, which was propped up by government price support programs, to a new crop contract, which was subject to revised agricultural legislation). If this price series were used for system testing, it would imply a mammoth profit for shorts (loss for longs) on the rollover day where in fact no such equity change would have been realized in actual trading.

Although the example provided represents a particularly extreme price gap at contract rollover, price gaps wide enough to cause significant distortions are quite common. The bottom line is that nearest futures can never be used for system testing.

## CONSTANT FORWARD ("PERPETUAL")

The constant-forward (also known as "perpetual") price series consists of quotes for prices a constant amount of time forward. The interbank currency market and the

London Metals Exchange markets provide actual examples of constant-forward price series. For example, the three-month forward price series for the Swiss franc represents the quote for the Swiss franc three months forward from each given day in the series. This is in contrast to the standard U.S. futures contract, which specifies a fixed expiration date.

A constant-forward series can be constructed from futures price data through interpolation. For example, if we were calculating a 90-day constant-forward (or perpetual) series, and the 90-day forward date fell exactly one-third of the way between the expirations of the nearest two contracts, the constant-forward price would be calculated as the sum of two-thirds of the nearest contract price and one-third of the subsequent contract price. As we moved forward in time, the nearer contract would be weighted less, but the weighting of the subsequent contract would increase proportionately. Eventually, the nearest contract would expire and drop out of the calculation, and the constant-forward price would be based on an interpolation between the subsequent two contracts.

The constant forward price series eliminates the problem of huge price gaps at rollover points and is certainly a significant improvement over a nearest futures price series. However, this type of series still has major drawbacks. To begin, it must be stressed that one cannot literally trade a constant-forward series, since the series does not correspond to any real contract. An even more serious deficiency of the constant-forward series is that it fails to reflect the effect of the evaporation of time that exists in actual futures contracts. This deficiency can lead to major distortions—particularly in carrying-charge markets.

To illustrate this point, consider a hypothetical situation in which spot gold prices remain stable at approximately $400/ounce for a one-year period, while forward futures maintain a constant premium of 1.0%, per two-month spread (see **Figure** 8-10). Given these assumptions, at each expiration, futures would converge to the unchanged spot price, losing $4 on the trade. The new futures contract would then be implemented at a price $4 higher that spot (as well as the expiring futures contract), and the whole process would be repeated. By the end of the year futures would lose a total of $24 ($2,400 per contract). Note, however, that the constant-forward series would completely fail to reflect this bear trend because it would register an approximate constant price. For example, a two-month constant-forward series would remain stable at approximately $404/ounce (1.01 x $400 = $404). Thus, the price pattern of a constant-forward series can easily deviate substantially from the pattern exhibited by the actual traded contracts—a highly undesirable feature.

As a final word, it should be noted that the problem just detailed regarding constant forward prices exists even when trading markets quoted as constant forward prices. The price series of these markets, in effect, reflect a different contract each day. For example, the 90-day forward position implemented today becomes an 89-day forward price tomorrow, not the quoted 90-day forward price. Therefore, the profit/loss of trades in these markets will also not be the same as that implied by the price series, which represents a constant forward quote.

## CONTINUOUS (SPREAD-ADJUSTED) PRICE SERIES

The spread-adjusted futures series, which we term "continuous futures," is constructed in such a way as to eliminate distortions due to the price gaps between expiring and subsequent futures contracts at transition points. In constructing a continuous futures price, the trader needs to specify two items of information:

1. The contract months used to construct the series (either all contract months traded for the given market, or some subset);
2. The rollover date or rollover rule (e.g., roll 20 days before last trading day, roll to the next contract when its 3-day average volume is greater than the corresponding volume for the current contract).

These items should be specified to correspond to actual trading. For example, if a trader in the cotton market trades only the March, July, and December contracts, the continuous futures series should be based only on these contracts and not all contracts. Similarly, if a trader normally rolls out of the old contract to the new contract on the $15^{th}$ calendar day (or next business day) before the contract month, the continuous futures series should use the same roll date. Again, the same general principal indicated in Cardinal Rule #4 applies: Test systems in a way that reflects the way they will actually be traded.

The continuous futures series will exactly reflect the equity of a long position consistently rolled over to the specified contract on the specified date. Therefore, profit/loss changes in continuous futures will exactly match changes in actual trading (assuming months and rollover dates are selected to correspond to actual trading).

Continuous futures data is available from a number of vendors. For most users, it will make much more sense to purchase continuous futures price series rather than to construct such series from contract price data. However, it is nonetheless helpful to go through a detailed example of how a continuous futures price series is constructed in order to better understand the concept of continuous futures.

**Figure** 8-11 illustrates the construction of a continuous futures price for the gold market. Note that this example uses hypothetical price data to simplify the illustration. Also, for simplicity of exposition, this illustration employs only two contract months, June and December; however, a continuous price could be formed using any number of traded contract months. For example, the continuous futures price could be constructed using the February, April, June, August, October, and December COMEX gold contracts.

For the moment, ignore the last column in **Figure** 8-11 and focus instead on the unadjusted continuous futures price (column 6). At the start of the period, the actual price and the unadjusted continuous futures price are identical. At the first rollover point, the forward contract (December 1992) is trading at a $6.00 premium to the nearby contract. All subsequent prices of the December 1992 contract are then adjusted downward by this amount (the addition of a negative nearby/forward spread), yielding the unadjusted continuous futures prices indicated in column 6. At the next rollover point, the forward contract (June 1993) is trading at a $4.00 premium to the nearby contract (December 1992). As a result, all subsequent actual prices of the June 1993 contract must now be adjusted by the cumulative adjustment factor—the total of all rollover gaps up to that point (−$10.00)—in order to avoid any artificial price gaps at the rollover point. This cumulative adjustment factor is indicated in column 5. The unadjusted continuous futures price is obtained by adding the cumulative adjustment factor to the actual price.

The preceding process is continued until the current date is reached (the intervening calculations are not shown). At this point, the final cumulative adjustment factor (which is a negative number) is subtracted from all the unadjusted continuous futures prices (column 6). This step sets the current price of the series equal to the price of the current contract—December 1998 in our example (recall that this example is using hypothetical price data)—without changing the shape of the series. This continuous futures price is indicated in column 7 of **Figure** 8-11. Note that although actual prices seem to imply a net price rise of $75 during the period surveyed, the continuous futures price indicates that prices actually declined by $25—the actual equity change that would have been realized by a constant long futures position.

In effect, the construction of the continuous series can be thought of as the equivalent of cutting out the price gap between the contracts on the rollover date and pasting the ends together. For example, **Figure** 8-12 compares the previously illustrated nearest futures cotton chart that exhibited the enormous price gap between the two contracts and the continuous futures equivalent.

In some markets, the spreads between nearby and forward contracts will range from premiums to discounts (for example, cattle). However, in other markets, the spread differences will be unidirectional. For example, in the gold market, the forward month always trades at a premium to the nearby month. In these types of markets, the spread-adjusted continuous price series will become increasingly disparate from actual prices.

It should be noted that in markets in which nearby premiums at contract rollovers tend to swamp nearby discounts, it is entirely possible for the series to eventually include negative prices for some past periods as cumulative adjustments mount. For example, during 1987–1991, there was a strong proclivity for nearby months in copper futures to trade at premiums to more forward contracts, often by wide margins. As a result, the price gain that would have been realized by a continuously held long futures position during this period far exceeded the net price gain implied by nearest futures, and the subtraction of the cumulative adjustment factor from current (1998) prices would result in negative prices for most of the 1980s (see **Figure** 8-13). Such an outcome is unavoidable if the continuous futures price series is to reflect the net gain in a continually held long position and if the series is shifted by the constant factor necessary to set the current continuous futures price equal to the current contract actual price.

Although the fact that a continuous futures price series could include negative prices may sound disconcerting, it does not present any problems in using the series for testing systems. The reason for this is that in measuring the profits or losses of trades, it is critical that the price series employed accurately reflects price *changes*, not price *levels*.

## SUMMARY: COMPARING PRICE SERIES

It is important to understand that a linked futures price series can only accurately reflect either price levels, as does nearest futures, or price moves as does continuous futures, but not both—much as a coin can either land on heads or tails, but not both. The adjustment process used to construct continuous series means that past prices in a continuous series will not match the actual historical prices that prevailed at the time. However, the essential point is that the continuous series is the only linked futures series that will exactly reflect price swings and hence equity fluctuations in an actual trading account (see **Figure** 8-14). Consequently, it is the only linked series that can be used to generate accurate simulations in computer testing of trading systems.

Are there any drawbacks to the continuous futures time series? Of course. It may be the best solution to the linked series problem, but it is not a perfect answer. A perfect alternative simply does not exist. One potential drawback, which is a consequence of the fact that continuous futures only accurately reflect price swings, not price levels, is that continuous futures cannot be used for any type of percentage calculations. This situation, however, can be easily remedied. If a system requires the calculation of a percentage change figure, use continuous futures to calculate the nominal price change and nearest futures for the divisor.

Another potential problem with continuous futures is that there is some unavoidable arbitrariness involved in constructing a continuous series, since one must decide which contracts to use and on what dates the rollovers should occur. However, this is not really a problem since these choices should merely mirror the contracts and rollover dates used in actual trading. Moreover, there is arbitrariness involved in the use of any of the price series discussed. A final problem is that, in some markets, the contracts being linked together may have very different past price patterns (for example, this is often the case in livestock markets). However, this problem would exist in any kind of linked series.

It should be emphasized that the price patterns of nearest futures and continuous futures can be strikingly different—to the degree one would not even know they represent the same market without a chart label. Consider, for example, **Figure** 8-15, which compares the cattle nearest futures chart with the continuous futures chart for the same market. Note that whereas the nearest futures chart implies the market witnessed a wide-swinging trading range pattern, perhaps even with a downward bias, the continuous futures chart makes clear that prices were in a strong bull market for most of the period. The experience of traders in this market would have corresponded to the continuous futures chart, not the nearest futures chart. As another example, **Figure** 8-16 compares the nearest and continuous futures charts in the cocoa market. Note that whereas the nearest futures chart implies that prices were in a general uptrend from 1992 forward, the continuous futures chart demonstrates that the price trend was actually down. In other words, during this period, it is the shorts that would have made money—in direct contrast to the implications of the nearest futures chart.

For the purpose of computer testing of trading systems, there are only two types of valid price series: (1) individual contract series, and (2) continuous futures series. Individual contract series are only a viable approach if the methodologies employed do not require looking back more than a few months in time (a restriction that rules out a vast number of technical approaches). In addition, the use of individual contract series is far clumsier. Thus, for most purposes, the continuous futures price series provides the best alternative. As long as one avoids using continuous prices for percentage calculations, this type of price series will yield accurate results (that is, results that parallel actual trading) as well as provide the efficiency of a single series per market. The constant-forward series, which is proposed by some as a method for linking prices, will create distortions rather than avoid them.

# LESSON 9: SELECTING THE TIME PERIOD AND PORTFOLIO

## DEFINING THE TIME PERIOD

If the time period over which a system is tested is not sufficiently long, the results may be unrepresentative and statistically unreliable. **Figure** 9-1 shows the performance table for a 15/150 crossover moving average system applied to Philip Morris for the years 1985-1997. For reasons explained in Lesson 7, we use a version of the system that trades a constant $1,000 per trade (i.e., number of shares = $1000/price) as opposed to 1 share (or some other constant number of shares) per trade. The total profit is $2229, and the profit factor is 2.92.

**Figure** 9-2 shows the same system applied to the same market for a broader time period: 1975-1997. Note that despite the much longer time period, the total net profit drops sharply to $1,300, while the profit factor is exactly halved to 1.46. As implied by these statistics, the portion of the broader time period prior to 1985 (1975-1984) is actually a significant net loser (see **Figure** 9-3). The explanation for the extremely disparate performance between 1975-1884 and 1985-1997 is that the latter period was dominated by many large trends (**Figure** 9-4 provides a typical example), while the earlier period was characterized by very choppy price behavior (**Figure** 9-5 provides a typical example).

The point of the foregoing example is that it is important to test a system over a broad enough time period to include all types of market phases. This is one reason for making test periods as long as possible. However, there is a counter argument that if the test period is too long, the early data may not be representative of the current market. The best solution is to test the system over as long a period as possible and then break out the results by time segments. In this manner, one can give greater weight to more recent periods, if so desired, while still being alerted to the fact if a system performed far worse in earlier years.

Except for short-term systems, it is advisable to use at least 15 years of price data in testing futures markets and at least 30 years in testing stocks (because of the extremely protracted bull market in stocks in recent history). Again, these results can be broken down by time periods, so that the more recent history can be analyzed independently.

## SINGLE VERSUS MULTIPLE MARKET SYSTEMS

Should systems be developed for each market independently or should the same system be used for a broad group of unrelated markets? There is no absolute answer to this question. The following are some of the key advantages and disadvantages of each approach:

**Single Market Advantages:**

Markets may have their own unique characteristics, which can only be captured by single market systems.

Some systems can only be developed for individual markets (e.g., those using fundamental data).

**Single Market Disadvantages:**

There is a great danger of *curvefitting* (fitting the system rules to past data) in single market systems. As a related point, testing results for single market systems are far less statistically reliable. In fact, because of the statistical reliability issue, probably only *short-term* systems can be tested for single markets, since for long-term systems, there will not be enough out-of-sample data to meaningfully test the system. ("Out-of-sample" data refers to data not used in developing the system.)

Designing a separate system for each market requires much more work.

**Multiple Market Advantages:**

One can have much more confidence in system results based on multimarket testing. For example, by developing a system on one market and then testing it on a group of other markets, it is possible to completely eliminate the danger of curvefitting. Also, multimarket testing provides far more data, giving the results significantly greater statistical reliability.

It is far more efficient to design the same system for many markets.

**Multiple Market Disadvantages:**

Certain approaches, such as any system using fundamental data, cannot be applied to multiple markets.

If markets have their own unique characteristics, a multimarket approach will throw away this information.

## DIVERSIFICATION

Should you diversify? Unless you feel confident that you can predict which market will do best in the *future*, the answer is a resounding "yes." In fact, it is possible for diversification to be beneficial even if the best return market in the *future* could be predicted. Why? Because risk could drop more than return—implying leverage could be used to get higher return at the same risk level.

To illustrate this concept, we apply a typical trend-following system (the 10/100 crossover moving average) to a group of 10 markets and compare the performance results of the individual markets versus a portfolio consisting of all the markets for the years 1984-1997. The portfolio is selected to represent different sectors: interest rates (T-bonds, Eurodollars), currencies (Deutsche mark, Japanese yen), metals (gold), energy (crude oil), grains (corn), livestock (cattle), and miscellaneous agricultural markets (sugar, cotton). The number of contracts assumed to be traded in each of these markets is adjusted to approximately equalize the volatility differences between the markets. Thus, for example, it is assumed that five times as many corn contracts are traded as T-bond contracts, because T-bonds were approximately five times as volatile as corn during the survey period. A $1 million account is assumed for each market and the portfolio in order to avoid fractional contracts when the portfolio is formed. However, the same basic principals would apply to much smaller account sizes.

Initially, we assume that the portfolio trades one-tenth the number of contracts as each single market (because there are 10 markets). **Figure** 9-6 compares the average return of the portfolio with the average annual returns of the individual markets. As can be seen, the portfolio returns are actually below the *median* return and far below the best market. (By definition, the return of the portfolio will equal the *average* of the single market numbers.) Where is the diversification benefit?

The answer is that you can't look at return alone. It is absolutely critical to also consider risk. **Figure** 9-7 ranks the markets and portfolio in ascending order of maximum drawdown. The maximum drawdown is the maximum equity decline from a peak to a low. As can be seen in **Figure** 9-7, the maximum drawdown of the portfolio is dramatically lower than the maximum drawdowns of the individual markets: less than one-third of the lowest individual market maximum drawdown.

As an aside, it should be noted that the maximum drawdown figures shown in **Figure** 9-7 and other tables in this study are based on month-end numbers only, but also include drawdowns of open profits. Generally speaking, the maximum drawdown calculated using this definition would be greater than the maximum intraday drawdown in TradeStation, which is based on daily numbers, but doesn't include the drawdown of open profits. (The TradeStation drawdown figure is calculated from the trade entry point not the equity peak.)

Maximum drawdown represents only a single event. Therefore, we also compare risk measured by the average drawdown. The average drawdown is the average of the monthly maximum drawdowns, with each month's maximum drawdown being defined as the decline from the prior equity peak. In other words, each monthly maximum drawdown represents the amount that would have been lost as of the end of that month if trading had commenced at the worst possible prior point. The average drawdown is derived by the following two-step process:

1. For each month, the difference between the prior equity peak and that month's ending equity is calculated.
2. These monthly differences are then averaged to yield the average drawdown.

**Figure** 9-8 ranks the markets and portfolio in ascending order of the average drawdown. Note that based on this measure, the risk of the portfolio is less than one-fifth of the lowest individual market number.

Thus far, we have seen that the profits of the portfolio are below the median, but that the risk is much lower. The key question is: How does the return/risk ratio of the portfolio compare with the return/risk ratios for the individual markets? **Figure** 9-9 shows that the return/maximum drawdown ratio for the portfolio is more than double the highest ratio for an individual market. **Figure** 9-10 indicates very similar results using the return/average drawdown ratio, with the portfolio ratio being more than double the highest market ratio. The implication of these statistics is that the portfolio can be traded at much greater leverage because its risk is so much lower.

The idea that a lower risk investment can be traded at greater leverage is a critical concept. People often make the mistake of focusing only on returns. Many people miss the point that even though the return of an investment may be lower, if the risk is lower by an even greater amount, then leverage can be applied to obtain a *higher return* at the same or lower risk level.

**Figure** 9-11 compares the individual market returns to a portfolio return in which the portfolio now trades three-tenths instead of one-tenth of each single market. As can be seen, the return of the portfolio is now higher than the return of the best individual market. But what happens to risk if we triple leverage? **Figures** 9-12 and 9-13 show that even at triple leverage the maximum drawdown and average drawdown of the portfolio are still lower than the corresponding lowest figures for an individual market.

What if the portfolio is traded at five times leverage? **Figure** 9-14 shows that the return is now more than double the best individual market return. As for risk, at five times leverage, the maximum drawdown of the portfolio is at the median level (**Figure** 9-15), but the average drawdown of the portfolio is still lower than the lowest individual market figure (**Figure** 9-16). **Figures** 9-17, 9-18 and 9-19 compare the cumulative equity of the portfolio versus the three best and three worst markets (other markets deleted to avoid clutter) for various leverage assumptions. Note how much smoother the portfolio equity curve is at no leverage and how much greater return is at five times leverage with smoothness still comparing well to single markets.

The foregoing tables and charts imply that in the given example the portfolio could have been traded at three to five times the leverage of individual markets, achieving a return well above the single best market with a well-below-average risk level. This is true even though the portfolio contained some losing and mediocre performing markets. In fact, in our particular example, even if a trader in the past had a crystal ball that accurately predicted which of the 10 markets was going to be the best performer in the future, he still could have achieved a higher return, at the equivalent risk level, trading the multimarket portfolio! In other words, diversification often makes it possible for the trader to achieve returns nearly equivalent (or sometimes even better) than the best performing markets. This is a tremendously important point, since it is obviously impossible to predict which will be the best performing market(s) in the future.

The study just presented was not a carefully chosen example, but was in fact the first example I constructed to illustrate the advantage of diversification. However, by chance, the results in this example were so powerful that I feel it is necessary to caution that you should not necessarily expect the portfolio to routinely outperform the single best market. (Remember, the best market can only be identified after the fact). Nevertheless, you can expect that, in most cases, the performance of the portfolio should at least be equivalent to the top tier of individual markets. Also, it should be noted that stock portfolios would not show as dramatic a diversification effect because individual stocks are likely to be much more correlated than the diverse group of futures in our example.

There are three key benefits to diversification:

1. **Dampened equity retracements**—As demonstrated in the preceding study, besides directly reducing risk, by dampening equity retracements, diversification makes it possible to achieve higher returns at equal to lower risk levels.

2. **Ensure participation in major moves**—Typically, at least for trend-following approaches in the futures markets, most of the profits in any given year are due

to only a few markets. In futures trading, missing only one or two of the major price moves could mean the difference between a very good year and a mediocre (or even losing) year. Trading a broad group of markets increases the chances of participating in any huge profit opportunity that might emerge.

3. **Bad luck insurance**— Although, over the long run, the net influence of luck on performance will be moderate to small, for any given trade, or small number of trades, luck can have an enormous impact on performance results. Futures systems trading, like baseball, is a game of inches. Given the right combination of circumstances, even a minute difference in the price movement on a single day could have an extraordinary impact on profit/loss.

To illustrate this point, we consider a 20-day breakout system with a confirmation rule requiring a close that penetrates the previous day's high (low) by a minimum amount. In System A, this amount is 5 points; in System B, it is 10 points. This is the only difference between the two systems. **Figure** 9-20 compares these two systems for the July 1981 coffee market. (Although more recent illustrations could easily have been used, this particular situation provides the most striking example I have ever encountered of the sensitivity of system performance to minute changes in the system values.)

The basic system buy signal (i.e., close above the 20-day high) was received on July 16. This buy was confirmed by System A on July 17 as the close was 9 points above the previous day's high ("A" Signal). System B, however, which required a 10-point penetration, did not confirm the signal until the following day ("B" Signal). The buy signal for system A would have been executed at approximately 97 cents ("A" Entry). However, due to the ensuing string of limit moves, the buy signal for system B could not be filled until prices surpassed $1.22 ("B" Entry). During this short interim, system A gained 25¢/lb ($9,375 per contract), while system B, which was unable to reverse its short position, lost a similar amount. Thus, the failure of the market to close one point higher on a given day (a price move equivalent to less than $4) resulted in an incredible $18,750 per contract difference in the performance of the two nearly identical systems!

The fewer the markets one trades, the greater the potential impact of luck—for better or worse—over the short run. And as the preceding example demonstrated, even minute price differences can sometimes have an enormous impact on profit/loss. In this respect, diversification helps reduce the potential influence of luck on performance.

As a final word, it should be noted that diversification can be employed even if one is trading single market systems. In this case, diversification can be achieved by trading several systems for the same market.

## PORTFOLIO ALLOCATION

The frequently used equal contract (share) allocation makes no sense. Although the illogic of this approach is more evident is stocks—the flaw of trading the same number of shares in a $10 stock as a $100 stock is obvious—the approach is equally invalid in futures. For stocks, a reasonable starting assumption is that individual stocks are traded in equal dollar amounts (e.g., 1,000 shares for a $10 stock and a 100 shares for a $100 stock). If desired, these equal dollar allocations may then be adjusted by some of the factors cited below.

The following factors should be considered in assigning contract allocation:

**Account Size**—Obviously, the greater the account size, the larger the number of contracts that can be traded in each market. (Of course, small increases in account size may not increase the number of contracts traded, since contracts can't be traded in fractional units.)

**Relative Volatilities**—Fewer contracts should be traded in markets with large average daily moves (measured in dollars per contract), such as coffee, than in markets with small average daily price moves, such as corn. (Note that *volatility* as used here is a function of both volatility and contract size. Also note that the equal dollar allocation assumption in stocks removes the main factor responsible for different average daily moves—the price level.)

**Relative Correlations**—If two highly correlated markets are traded (e.g., T-bonds and T-notes), their relative allocation should be reduced vis-à-vis two completely unrelated markets.

**Sporadic High Risk Markets**—Markets that tend to witness sporadic periods of abrupt, steep increases in volatility (e.g., Mexican peso) should probably be traded at a lower allocation than implied by the market's recent volatility.
Relative Performance Expectations –Traders may wish to assign greater allocations to markets that have performed better in the past if they expect this relative performance pattern to persist in the future.

Contract allocations should be determined prior to *system* testing. It may be useful to first determine percent allocations to each market and then to translate these percentages into number of contracts.

# LESSON 10: MODIFICATIONS FOR TREND-FOLLOWING SYSTEMS — CONFIRMATION CONDITIONS

A confirmation condition is a condition that must be met before a signal is taken. Thus, if a buy or sell signal is received, instead of automatically taking the signal, one monitors for a confirmation condition. The trade is only taken if the confirmation condition is fulfilled before an opposite direction signal is received. The purpose of a confirmation condition is to reduce the number of false signals. One downside of confirmation conditions is that they normally result in worse entries on valid signals. In this lesson, we will explore several different types of confirmation conditions.

**PENETRATION OF THRESHOLD CONFIRMATION**

This type of confirmation condition requires that the market exceed some price threshold before the signal is taken. **Figure** 10-1 illustrates a 30-day breakout system with an average daily true range (ADTR) confirmation condition. The ADTR was defined in Lesson 3. In this system, a buy signal requires a two step process (sell signals are analogous):

1. a close above the prior 30-day high (similar to a basic breakout system);
2. a close greater than the close in step 1 + 3*ADTR.

Of course, the number 3 in the second condition is a parameter of the system, as is the number of days in the breakout is step 1.

The top chart in **Figure** 10-1 shows the signals of the basic breakout system and the thresholds that must be reached on a close in order to confirm the signals. The lower chart shows the confirmed signals only. For example, in early March 1990, the basic system generates a buy signal. The system using the confirmation condition does not take this buy signal until early April when prices close above the threshold, which lies 3*ADTR above the basic system signal. In this case, using the confirmation condition results in a worse entry and therefore has a negative impact on performance.

In May 1990, the basic system generates a sell signal. In this instance, however, the market never closes below the threshold level defined by the confirmation condition. Thus, the system using the confirmation condition sidesteps the losing trade in May 1990, making money in the interim until the next buy signal, whereas the basic system realizes a loss. Note that the subsequent buy signal in late June 1990 is ignored by the system using the confirmation condition because it is already long. In similar fashion, the confirmation condition helps avoid the losing September 1990 signal.

## TIME DELAY CONFIRMATION

This type of confirmation condition requires that the market close above (below) the original buy (sell) signal after a minimum wait period. **Figure** 10-2 illustrates this type of system using the same 30-day breakout and a wait period of 5 days. Therefore, instead of automatically taking a buy signal, one waits for 5 days and then goes long if the market closes above the original buy signal price before a breakout sell signal is received. (The sell case would be analogous.)

The top chart in **Figure** 10-2 shows the signals of the basic breakout system and the signal prices that must be exceeded by a close 5 days or more after the signal. The lower chart shows the confirmed signals only. The early March 1990 buy signal was confirmed when the market closed above the original breakout level after the 5-day wait period. The subsequent losing sell signal in May 1990 was filtered as the market failed to close below the signal price after the 5-day wait period. The subsequent late June 1990 buy signal was ignored because the system was already long. In this case, however, the losing September 1990 sell signal was taken as the market closed just below the original sell signal exactly 5 days later.

## PATTERN CONFIRMATION

In this type of system, a chart pattern is used to confirm the original signal. The example provided uses the concept of a thrust day. An up thrust day is a day with a close above the previous day's high; a down thrust day is a day with a close below the previous day's low. The confirmation condition consists of the requirement that the market witness a certain number of thrust days (5 in or example) beyond the signal price. **Figure** 10-3 provides a close-up illustration of this confirmation condition for the same 30-day breakout system used in the preceding examples. The dashed line represents the original signal price (i.e., the close that exceeded the previous 30-day high). The first 5 up thrust days above this line are marked. The $5^{th}$ such day fulfills the confirmation condition for the trade.

The top chart in **Figure** 10-4 shows the signals of the basic breakout system and the signal prices that must be exceeded by 5 thrust days. The lower chart shows the confirmed signals only. The early March 1990 buy signal, which was shown in close-up in **Figure** 10-3, was confirmed. The subsequent losing sell signals in May and September 1990 were filtered, however, as the market failed to witness 5 down thrust days below these signal levels. Thus as can be seen in the lower chart, the market remained long throughout the period illustrated once the March buy signal was confirmed.

The basic trade-off intrinsic in a confirmation condition is that it will help avoid some whipsaws at the expense of worse entries on valid signals. Although, in the above three examples, the benefits of the confirmation condition significantly outweighed its adverse impact, the net balance between these contrasting influences must be determined on a case-by-case basis by testing. The results will vary dependent on the specific system, the specific confirmation condition, the markets tested, and the time period used for testing.

## LESS SENSITIVE PARAMETERS AS ALTERNATIVE TO CONFIRMATION CONDITION

In the previous examples, the confirmation condition reduced whipsaws at the expense of worse entries. A similar effect can be achieved by using less sensitive parameters. For example, **Figure** 10-5 compares the 30-day breakout system used in the previous examples with a 60-day breakout system. Note that the less sensitive parameter avoids the May and September whipsaw sell signals at the expense of a worse entry on the profitable March buy signal, which with N=60 is delayed until April. In this sense, the use of less sensitive parameters can often be used as a viable alternative to confirmation conditions. Nevertheless, confirmation conditions provide another tool for constructing systems and may sometimes provide a better approach.

# LESSON 11: MODIFICATIONS FOR TREND-FOLLOWING SYSTEMS — TRADE SIGNAL FILTER, DIFFERENTIATION BETWEEN BUY AND SELL SIGNALS, & PYRAMIDING

## TRADE SIGNAL FILTER

As the name implies, filters are used to filter out trade signals that exhibit or fail to exhibit certain conditions on the hypothesis that those trades have a lower probability of success. **Figure** 11-1 provides an example of a filter. This system uses a 40-day breakout to enter into trades and then liquidates the position after 30 days (assuming an opposite direction breakout has not occurred first). After liquidation, trades can be re-entered in the same direction on a new breakout signal. However, after a sufficient length of time has elapsed without an opposite direction breakout, we may no longer wish to re-enter the trade on a new breakout, on the premise that the market may be overdue for a reaction. This system uses a filter based on this premise. Specifically, breakout signals that occur after more than 100 days have elapsed without an intervening opposite direction breakout signal are filtered (i.e., not taken).

The top chart in **Figure** 11-1 shows the trades generated by the system without the filter rule. The lower chart depicts the signals for the same system, using the 100-day rule filter. As can be seen, the July, September, and October 1984 buy signals occur in both versions. However, the January 1985 buy signal is filtered because more than 100 days have elapsed since the first breakout buy signal in the sequence without an intervening downside breakout signal.

A filter could be any of the following:
- fundamental or technical;
- based on action in another market (e.g., T-bond as filter for S&P);
- based on prior trades;
- based on relative performance (e.g., only take a buy signal in a stock if the stock has outperformed the stock index based on some specified measure).

Note that a rejected signal can sometimes be taken at a later point if the condition is met *before* an opposite signal occurs. For example, if a stock index system uses a trend measure of the bond market as a filter (i.e., eliminates stock index signals that are opposite the bond market trend), a reversal of the bond trend could activate a stock signal that was originally filtered. (In the preceding example of a filter, however, once a trade is filtered—more than 100 days have elapsed without an opposite direction breakout—it is permanently eliminated.) Also note that signals that occur after filtered signals are ignored, because the net position is already consistent with the implied trade (assuming system that is always in market).

The distinction between a confirmation condition and a filter is that a filter is a screening rule applied *at the time of the basic signal,* while a confirmation condition is a requirement that must be met *after the basic signal is received.* Thus a system could have both a filter and a confirmation condition.

## DIFFERENTIATION BETWEEN BUY AND SELL SIGNALS

In some circumstances, it may be desirable to differentiate between buy and sell signals. Some examples include:

In applying a system to the stock market, we may want to take only buy signals. Alternatively, in applying a system to the stock market, we may want to require more stringent conditions for a sell than for a buy.
In non-financial futures markets, it might be reasonable to use more sensitive conditions for sells on the premise that markets fall quicker than they rise.

It should be emphasized, however, that differentiating between buy and sell signals increases the danger of curvefitting. Therefore, any trader using such an approach should be particularly cognizant of this potential pitfall.

## PYRAMIDING

**Figure** 11-2 shows a buy signal generated by a breakout system with N=100. Although this was great signal, capturing a huge price advance, the system failed to fully exploit the subsequent upmove because it did not add to the original position. The addition of positions to an original position (called the *base position*) is called *pyramiding*. The rationale for pyramiding is to take greater advantage of long, sustained trends. Since there is a significant danger of assuming excessive risk when pyramiding, it is important that any pyramiding strategy incorporate risk control rules.

**Figure** 11-3 illustrates a pyramid strategy applied to a 100-day breakout system. This strategy requires four conditions to be met before adding to an original position:

The initial requirement is a pullback in the trend, which is defined as a short-term (e.g., 10-day) breakout in the opposite direction (e.g., a downside breakout if the base position is long).

This development must be followed by a resumption of the trend, which is defined as a short-term (e.g., 10-day) breakout in the direction of the existing position.

Once the second condition is met, a pyramid unit is then added if the previous position (base or pyramid) has a profit.
The maximum position (base plus pyramid) is limited to a specified number (e.g., 3).

To see how this system works, let's step through the trades in **Figure** 11-3. A 100-day upside breakout provides a base unit buy signal in September 1979. The market then witnesses a 10-day downside breakout and a subsequent 10-day upside breakout. However, since the base long position has a loss when the 10-day upside breakout occurs (November 1979), a pyramid unit is not added. (In other words, condition 3 is not fulfilled at this point.) A subsequent 10-day downside breakout followed by a 10-day upside breakout results in adding a pyramid unit (second unit overall) in early January 1980. In this case, the pyramid position is added because the base position is at a profit. Ironically, in this instance, the pyramid strategy performs terribly, adding a second unit at the virtual top of the market.

The subsequent market decline leads to a 100-day downside breakout at the end of February 1980, which prompts the liquidation of the entire long position and the initiation of a base short position. The first opposite direction (upside) 10-day breakout occurs in April 1980, fulfilling the first condition for adding a pyramid unit. The first subsequent 10-day downside breakout occurs at the end of July 1980. Since the base unit has a profit at this point and the total position is less than three, a pyramid unit is added.

A second pyramid unit (third unit overall) is added in September 1980 following a 10-day upside breakout in early September and then a 10-day downside breakout, with the second unit showing a profit at this point. Since the total position size is equal to three at this point (the limit specified by condition 4), the system ceases to monitor for any additional pyramid units. As **Figure** 11-4 illustrates, the implementation of this third unit is followed by a long slide. In this particular instance, the inclusion of a pyramid strategy substantially enhances profits. However, the pyramid strategy can also result in increased losses, as is the case in example provided by **Figure** 11-5.

In the pyramid strategy just illustrated, pyramid positions, as well as the base position, are liquidated by an opposite direction base signal (i.e., 100-day breakout). However, in order to limit the potential loss on pyramid positions, it may be desirable to add additional conditions (besides an opposite direction base signal) for liquidating pyramid positions. **Figure** 11-6 illustrates a system that adds pyramid unit stop loss rules to the breakout/pyramid strategy system just detailed. In this system, *all* pyramid units are liquidated when either:

there is an opposite direction base signal (as was the case in the previous system), or there is an opposite direction short-term (e.g., 10-day) breakout and the close on such a breakout results in the last pyramid unit being at a loss.

In **Figure** 11-6 there are two instances where pyramid units are liquidated by the second condition. In June 1989, a 10-day high close, which is also above the last sell entry, causes all pyramid units to be liquidated, thereby preventing a pyramid profit from turning into a loss. In February 1990 a 10-day low close, which is also below the previous buy entry, causes all pyramid units to be liquidated. In this latter case, however, the additional pyramid liquidation rule signals a premature exit and results in a lost profit opportunity.

# LESSON 12: MODIFICATIONS FOR TREND-FOLLOWING SYSTEMS — TRADE EXIT STRATEGIES

## STOPS: DEFINITIONS AND BASIC CONCEPTS

A stop is a point at which a position is liquidated in order to prevent a worse loss or to prevent a further surrender of open profits. In this sense, a stop on a long position will always be below the market and conversely a stop on a short position will always be above the market. (Note: sometimes stops are used to enter positions in the direction of the market movement—for example, a buy order placed above the market. In our discussion, however, we are only concerned with the use of stops for exiting positions.)

A *money management* stop is a stop used to limit the loss on a trade. A *trailing stop* is used to lock in an increasing profit on a trade. For example, if one is long and the market is rising, the stop may be periodically increased as the advance progresses, locking in a larger and larger profit.

Stops can be based on either price closes only or on intraday prices. If a system allows stop points to be triggered intraday, there are two important caveats:

1. The accurate testing of such a system requires intraday data.
2. Generally speaking, trades that are liquidated on intraday stops are likely to witness above-average slippage, a factor that should be incorporated into the transaction cost assumptions used in testing the system.

In TradeStation a variety of different stops can be incorporated into any trading system without any additional programming. This is but one example of how TradeStation tremendously simplifies the task of system programming vis-à-vis programming in conventional computer languages. By making a few dialog box selections, the desired stop strategy can be automatically added to a system. To bring up the appropriate dialog box, once the chart with the inserted system is on the screen, double click any buy/sell signal arrow and choose the Stops tab. (Alternatively, you could make the following menu selections: Format, Analysis Techniques, highlight system line, Format, select Stops tab.) These steps will bring up the dialog box shown in **Figure** 12-1. In this illustration, the money management stop option has been selected, and the dollar amount of the stop has been specified at $1,000. This means that any time a given trade is losing $1,000 per contract, it will be liquidated.

## STOPS: THE BASIC TRADE-OFF

There is a basic trade-off in using stops. On the positive side, stops can help limit losses. On the negative side, stops can also eliminate good trades, turning trades that would have been winners without a stop into losers. **Figure** 12-2 illustrates three consecutive trades in which the use of a $1,000 money management stop significantly reduced the losses on signals generated by a 12/120 crossover moving average system during a whipsaw period. However, as shown in **Figure** 12-3, immediately following this period, the stop rule caused the premature liquidation of a trade that turned out to be a huge winner.

How did the instances in which the stop rule helped balance out with the situations in which it was detrimental? **Figure** 12-4 compares the performance table for the 12/120 crossover moving average system run on the T-bond market for 1979-early 1998 with the performance table for the same system with a $1,000 money management stop. Note that the use of this stop rule dramatically reduces the total profit and also reduces the return/risk measures, such as return on account and the profit factor. Apparently, at least in this example, the adverse impact of prematurely liquidating good trades significantly outweighed the benefit of reducing losses on losing trades.

## ADDING RE-ENTRY CONDITIONS

One problem with using a stop is that it could result in missing a major profit opportunity if the market reverses back to the original trend after the stop is hit and before the underlying system generates an opposite direction signal. For example, if a long position in a crossover moving average system is stopped out, and the market reverses back to the upside without any intervening downside crossover in the moving average, then there will not be an upside crossover to signal a re-entry into long side. Thus, in this type of situation, the use of a stop can result in missing a subsequent uptrend, no matter how large.

One method of dealing with this problem of missing major trading opportunities by using stops is to combine the use of stops with a re-entry condition. **Figure** 12-5 illustrates the same 12/120 crossover moving average system using a $1,000 money management stop with the addition of the following re-entry rule: If stopped out of a long position, re-enter long if the market closes above the highest high of the past 50 days; if stopped out of a short position, re-enter short if the market closes below lowest the low of past 50 days. In **Figure** 12-5, the re-entry rule actually makes matters worse by creating numerous whipsaws, as the system witnesses a phase in which it alternates between re-entry sells and money management stops. However, in **Figure** 12-6, which illustrates the same market in the following year, the re-entry rule gets the system back long after being stopped out for what proves to be a immense move. In this example, the large winning trades made possible by the re-entry rule far outweigh the far more numerous, but smaller, losses caused by this rule, as can be seen in the performance comparison in **Figure** 12-7.

## USING WIDER STOPS

Although wider stops, by definition, will result in worse losses on losing trades, they will also eliminate fewer good trades. This benefit can often outweigh the effect of larger losses on losing trades. **Figure** 12-8 illustrates the same 12/120 crossover moving average system using a $2,000 money management stop instead of the $1,000 stop previously used. In the initial period, the use of a wider stop results in worse losses on a sequence of losing trades. However, the use of a wider stop avoids knocking out the January 1982 buy, which proved to be a major winning trade. (This trade was stopped out using the $1,000 stop.) **Figure** 12-9 compares the performance of the system using a $1,000 stop with performance of the same system using a $2,000 stop. In this example, the wider stop's advantage of knocking out fewer good trades far outweighs the larger losses on losing trades. This particular example illustrates another cardinal rule:

> CARDINAL RULE 5: Excessive risk avoidance can be very expensive.

## BREAKEVEN STOPS

As the name implies, a break-even stop is intended to get out at the entry level once the trade is ahead. The break-even stop requires one input: the minimum open profit needed to activate the stop.

To incorporate a break-even stop into a system, once a chart with an inserted system is on screen, double click any buy/sell signal arrow, which will bring up the Format System dialog box, and choose the Stops tab. These steps will bring up the dialog box shown in **Figure**12-10. In this illustration, the floor for the break-even stop has been specified at $2,000. This means that at any point the trade has an open profit of $2,000 or more the break-even stop will be activated. If the market subsequently returns to the entry level, the trade will be liquidated.

It should be noted that the break-even stop would normally be used in addition to a money management stop; otherwise the risk would be open-ended if the minimum floor open profit needed to activate the break-even stop was not reached. The trade-off in using a break-even stop is that it transforms some losing trades into near break-even trades, but at the expense of eliminating some big wins that would not otherwise have been stopped out.

**Figure** 12-11 illustrates a break-even stop with a $2,000 floor applied to the 12/120 crossover moving average system. In this instance, the use of the break-even stop triggered the liquidation of a short position near the top of a minor rebound, thereby causing the system to miss a major profit opportunity. However, **Figure** 12-12 shows that in the subsequent period, the use of the break-even stop eliminated a sequence of whipsaw losses. On balance, in this example, the addition of the break-even stop significantly improved the return/risk measures. As can be seen in **Figure** 12-13, total profits are very similar with and without the breakeven stop; however, the return/risk measures, such as the profit factor and return on account, are significantly higher with the addition of the break-even stop. Of course, this single example does not prove anything, but a break-even stop is a strategy worth exploring, particularly for those traders who might find such an approach easier to follow in a disciplined manner.

## TRAILING STOPS

As the name implies, a trailing stop trails behind a position. For example, in the case of a long position, as the market rises, the stop is raised. TradeStation has two types of trailing stops: a dollar risk trailing stop and a percent risk trailing stop. The dollar risk trailing stop requires one input: the dollar amount of a retracement from the highest high if long (lowest low if short) that signals the liquidation of the position. For example, if the dollar risk is equal to $1,000, the position would be liquidated any time the trade retraced $1,000 from its most profitable point. The percent risk trailing stop requires two inputs and will be discussed and illustrated later in this lesson in the section, *Using Stops as Liquidation Rules for Buy Only Stock Systems*.

To incorporate a trailing stop into a system, once a chart with an inserted system is on screen, double click any buy/sell signal arrow, which will bring up the Format System dialog box, and choose the Stops tab. These steps will bring up the dialog box shown in **Figure** 12-14. In this illustration, the dollar risk trailing stop is selected and the dollar amount specified at $2,000.

The basic trade-off in using a trailing stop is that it will lock in open profits or limit losses at the expense of missing some profit opportunities. **Figures** 12-15 to 12-18 illustrates two different trailing stops applied to a 12/120 crossover moving average system in T-bonds. **Figure** 12-15 provides a typical example where the trailing stop improves performance by limiting the surrender of open profits, with the narrower stop doing better because it helps retain a larger portion of profits. **Figure** 12-16 shows an example where both trailing stops do much worse than the basic system by signaling a highly premature exit in what would otherwise have been an extremely profitable trade. **Figure** 12-17 provides an example where the narrower stop results in turning a potentially profitable trade into a net loser, whereas the wider stop avoids getting knocked out of the trade. It should be pointed out, however, that even when the wider stop avoids getting knocked out of a trade, capturing additional profits, it may get triggered at a latter point, and thereby still end up missing the bulk of profits (see **Figure** 12-18).

**Figure** 12-19 provides performance summaries for the two trailing stop versions. As can seen, in this example, the narrower trailing stop results in surrendering the bulk of the profits. Although, as always, a single example does not provide proof, generally speaking, if the trailing stop is set too low, it will get triggered easily and end up getting knocked out of most good trades. This trait will usually outweigh any profit retention or loss control advantages. The moral is that although narrow trailing stops may be tempting because they are parsimonious in surrendering open profits, they usually cause more than harm than good. This is another example of Cardinal Rule 5 stated earlier: Excessive risk avoidance can be very expensive.

## TIME STOPS

Thus far, we have discussed only money-based stops, or equivalently, stops based on price movement. In contrast, the time stop, as the name implies, is based on time as opposed to market movement. The basic premise of the time stop is that if the trade is good, it should be ahead after a specified number of days have elapsed.

**Figure** 12-20 shows the 12/120 crossover moving average system with a 40-day time stop applied to the corn market. This system will liquidate a trade anytime it has a close worse than the entry level after at least 40 days have elapsed from time of entry. In this illustration, the stop helps avoid a losing trade. In **Figure** 12-21, however, the use of the time stop results in missing a huge winning trade. In essence, the time stop has the same tradeoff as the other stops we have discussed: it will limit losses in some cases at the expense of missing good trades in other instances. The balance between these two contrasting influences would have to be gauged by testing.

## TIME STOPS WITH RE-ENTRY RULE

As is the case with other types of stops, re-entry rules can be added to system using time stops to avoid missing major trends. **Figure** 12-22 shows how adding a re-entry rule—replacing a stopped out short (long) position if the market closes below (above) the prior 50-day low (high)—manages to salvage the bulk of the profit potential that would have been lost by using a time stop without this rule. As before, although the use of a re-entry rule will prevent missing some major winning trades, it will also create some additional whipsaw losses. The balance between these contrasting influences will depend on the specific market, system, and parameter sets.

## DYNAMIC STOP RULES

Thus far, we have only discussed static stops (e.g., fixed money stop, fixed time stop). A dynamic stop, as the name implies, varies over time. One example of a dynamic stop would be a stop that is made more sensitive as open profits in a trade increase. Another type of dynamic stop is one that varies in line with changing volatility. In other words, when the market is more volatile, the stop would be wider than it would be if the market were less volatile.

The latter type of dynamic stop is depicted in **Figure** 12-23. In this illustration, the stop is linked to a multiple of the average daily true range. Specifically, the buy stop will be set equal to the lowest low plus six times the average daily true range, and the sell stop will be set equal to the highest high minus six times the average daily true range. Therefore, when the average daily true range widens, the stop will expand as well. As can be seen in **Figure** 12-23, when the average daily true range is relatively wide during the collapsing phase of the market, the stop is 39 cents above the lowest low. However, once the average daily true range contracts with the transition to a trading range market, the stop is only 18 cents above the lowest low.

In a conventional stop, the stop will be triggered at the extreme of the decline up to that point in time. The dynamic stop, however, can be triggered at significantly better levels than existed at earlier points of the retracement. For example, in **Figure** 12-24, note that decreasing volatility causes the stop to narrow significantly, with the result that the stop is hit at a much higher level than the low point of the decline.

## USING STOPS AS LIQUIDATION RULES FOR BUY ONLY STOCK SYSTEMS

In the stock market, the combination of a strong, upside bias in stock prices over the long-term and the difficulties involved in shorting stocks often make it desirable to design long-only trading systems. In this context, it should be noted that stop strategies can be combined with trend-following buy signals to form a stock trading system.

An example of such a system is described by the following rules:

The system goes long on a close above the prior 50-day high (i.e., a breakout buy signal).

Long positions are liquidated when either a money management stop or a percent trailing stop is hit. Since this is a stock trading system, as previously discussed, we assume that each trade is for a constant $1,000, with the number of shares in the trade adjusted accordingly. The money management stop is set equal to $50, which based on this assumption, implies a 5% stop level. The percent trailing stop has two components: (1) minimum gain needed to activate the stop, which is set to $400, a figure equivalent to a 40% gain, given the constant $1,000 trade size assumption; (2) a retracement level (from the highest open profit level) of 30%. The stop dialog box selections that correspond to these inputs are illustrated in **Figure** 12-25. (As before, this dialog box is accessed by double-clicking any buy/sell signal arrow and choosing the Stops tab.)

The system also includes a 50-wait rule—that is, a new long position cannot be implemented within 50 days of a previous long position being stopped out.

Various aspects of this system are illustrated in **Figure** 12-26 to 12-28. In **Figure** 12-26, a long position is liquidated when the trailing stop is hit. **Figure** 12-27 provides an example of the money management stop keeping the loss small on a buy signal that occurred at almost the exact market peak. **Figure** 12-28 provides an illustration of the 50-day wait rule preventing a buy signal from being generated when the market makes a new 50-day high. **Figure** 12-29 and 12-30 compare this system to the same system using a narrower money management stop (3%) and a wider trailing stop (50%). In **Figure** 12-29, the use of a wider trailing stop results in a much worse exit. However, in **Figure** 12-30, the wider trailing stop avoids getting knocked out of an excellent trade, which the system with the narrower trailing stop ends up re-entering at a significantly higher price level. Finally, **Figure** 12-31, which illustrates the 3%/50% stop combination system version applied to Dell, demonstrates that this system can sometimes capture an enormous price move, even though the initial maximum risk is very low (3%)

Even if a buy-and-hold strategy makes more money in the end, combining technical entry rules with a stop strategy still has the following advantages:

We don't know ahead of time, which stock will tank.

In the future, it is unlikely that the incredible bullish bias of the past 25 years will be duplicated.

Even stocks that skyrocket may have periods of terrible performance, and stops can avert disaster. (See, for example, **Figure** 12-32, which depicts Dell, the same stock shown in **Figure** 12-31, in an earlier year).

Investors starting out with the intention of using a buy-and-hold approach may bail out during a bad period before the stock rebounds.

Knowing that stops will limit the loss and the amount of profit surrendered may give investors the confidence to stay with a position longer than they would otherwise.

## USING PROFIT OBJECTIVES TO EXIT TRADE

As the name implies, profit objectives set a target at which profits are taken. For example, if the profit objective is $3,000, the trade would be liquidated any time it showed a profit of $3,000, even if the market was still trending steadily in the direction of the trade. Without passing judgment on its validity, the premise underlying the use of objectives is that if the market moves sufficiently in one direction, the odds of a retracement and hence a surrender of profits are enhanced. Profit objectives can be set in TradeStation by accessing the same dialog box used to set stops, selecting the profit target box and specifying the dollar amount (see **Figure 12-33**).

**Figure** 12-34 and 12-35 show the effects of adding a $3,000 profit objective to a 12/120 crossover moving average system applied to the silver market. As can be seen, the use of the profit objective provides a number of excellent exit signals, two of which occur at the virtual market turns. **Figures** 12-36 and 12-37 show the same system with a $4,000 profit objective applied to the British pound. In this case, the use of the profit objective results in drastically reducing the profit potential of winning trades.

Although profit objectives may be beneficial in wide-swinging, choppy markets (e.g., **Figures** 12-34 and 12-35), they will tend to dramatically reduce profits in trending markets (e.g., **Figures** 12-36 and 12-37). Generally speaking, using objectives will often hurt more than it helps, probably because using profit objectives violates the classic trading rule of letting profits run. However, this is an opinion, not an absolute fact. The intended message here is not that profit objectives should always be avoided, but rather that profit objectives should not be used without first testing their impact on the given system's performance. Traders who use objectives without such testing, might be surprised at the results. One possible alternative is to use extreme objectives that apply only rarely, but this approach won't help in choppy markets and could still give up some windfall profits

# LESSON 13: SYSTEM PROGRAMMING TECHNIQUES — EASYLANGUAGE BASICS

In all our discussions of system programming, we will use EasyLanguage. Because EasyLanguage was specifically designed for the purpose of developing trading systems and indicators, these tasks are far simpler in EasyLanguage than in conventional programming languages. The following presentation does not assume any prior knowledge of either programming in general or EasyLanguage in particular. Those with prior programming knowledge will find a great deal of similarity between EasyLanguage and counterpart concepts in other programming languages, such as C.

## CALCULATIONS THROUGH TIME

Perhaps the most basic concept to understand is that a program is applied one price bar at a time, moving through time. In other words, the computer will run through all the lines of a program (except those that are skipped by conditional instructions) for the first price bar, then move to the next bar and repeat the process, and so on through the last price bar.

## PRICE REFERENCES

All price bars are referenced relative to the current bar, with the number of bars prior to the current bar indicated in brackets. The current bar would be [0], which is optional (i.e., if there is no bracket term, it is assumed the reference is to the current bar). Thus, assuming daily data, the following are examples of references to price close data:
- Current Bar (today)—Close or C or Close[0] or C[0]
- Previous Bar (yesterday)—Close[1] or C[1]
- Bar 10 days ago—Close[10] or C[10]
- Bar N days ago—Close[N] or C[N]

Price references to the open (O), high (H), and low (L) would be analogous.

## SEMICOLONS

Every statement in EasyLanguage ends in a semicolon, analogous to the use of a period in written languages.

## MAXBARSBACK

An indicator or system cannot be applied beginning with the first bar on a chart, because a certain number of bars are needed to calculate all the expressions in the program. The MaxBarsBack refers to the minimum number of bars needed to calculate all the terms in a program. For example, in a simple crossover moving average system, with the moving average lengths set at 20 and 100 the MaxBarsBack would equal 100. This means that at least 100 bars of prior data would be required before the system could be applied. The Format System/Properties tab dialog box (accessed by double-clicking any buy/sell signal arrow or by clicking on Format—Analysis Techniques) contains a box for "maximum number of bars system will reference" (see **Figure** 13-1). This is where the MaxBarsBack value would be entered for a system. If this value is set too low, there will not be sufficient data set aside to perform the calculations required by the program, and an error message will be generated.

## PYRAMIDING OPTIONS

The Format System/Properties dialog box (**Figure** 13-1) also has a section for Pyramid Settings. There are 3 possible choices:

1. Do not allow entries in same direction
2. Allow multiple entries in the same direction by different entry signal
3. Allow multiple entries in the same direction by same and different entry signal

Typically, the first option will be selected. If this is the case, once the system generates a buy (sell) signal, subsequent repetitions of the conditions necessary for a buy (sell) signal will not result in an additional position. Selecting this first option will obviate the need to write lines of code to prevent more than one position in a given direction. For example, if this option is selected in a 50-day breakout system, after the first 50-day upside breakout, which reverses the system from short to long, subsequent occurrences of 50-day upside breakouts would be ignored, until an opposite entry occurs.

Sometimes, however, as was illustrated in an earlier lesson, we may have a system that deliberately allows pyramid positions. If this is the case, we would select the third option: "Allow multiple entries in same direction by same and different entry signals." If this option is chosen it is critical that some limit be placed on the maximum number of positions established. This constraint can be achieved in two ways: (1) by specifically including a maximum position size in the system (an example of this will be provided in a latter lesson), or (2) by entering this maximum in the dialog box in the Entry Settings section, in the line "Maximum open entries per position."

Why would we ever use the first approach, when the second method is obviously simpler? Because we may want the maximum position size to be a parameter in the system. If it is a parameter, we can test multiple parameter sets containing different values for the maximum position size at one time, as opposed to changing the dialog box each time the value is changed.

Thus far, we have not discussed the second option in the Pyramid Settings box. This option would be selected if our system had two or more sets of rules for generating buy (sell) signals, and we wanted to allow each entry method to generate a signal even if another entry method had already generated a signal in the same direction. Thus, as indicated in the setting selection, this option would "allow multiple entries in same direction by different signals."

## COMMENTS

Comments are enclosed in curly brackets: { }. Anything placed between curly brackets will be ignored by EasyLanguage. Comments are extremely useful as reminder notes to explain the programming code. When you first finish writing a program, the purpose of the program, as well as the individual sections of code in the program, will usually be pretty clear. However, if you write many programs and then go back to a particular program six months or more later, you may have totally forgotten exactly what the program does or the purpose of certain sections of the code. Of course, by carefully going over the code, you can certainly **FIGURE** it out, since you were the one who wrote it. However, it would be far easier to read summary commentaries.

I would advise always using comments, and moreover using comments liberally. The little bit of extra time required to write the comments when the program is fresh in your mind will save you multiples of time if you have to decipher this program at a later date. There are three types of comments that I recommend should be used in all but the simplest programs:

1. a summary description of the program (e.g., system, indicator);
2. a comment at the start of each section of code, briefly explaining what that section does;
3. an explanation of any part of the code you anticipate may be unclear if revisited in the future (including, where appropriate, an explanation of why that segment of code was necessary).

## INPUTS

In TradeStation and other Omega Research products, user-definable *parameters* are called system *inputs*. The two terms refer to identical concepts and are totally interchangeable. A parameter (input) is a value that can be freely assigned in a system in order to vary timing of signals. For example, the number of past days whose high must be exceeded to generate a buy signal in a breakout system is a parameter (input).

**Format:**

Inputs: Input Name (Initialization value), Input Name (Initialization value);

**Example:**

In a 10/80 crossover moving average system, the input statement line might read as follows (the names of the inputs—n1 and n2 in this example—can, of course, be different):

    Inputs: n1(10), n2(80);

**Key Point:**

Inputs are fixed (constant) for any run

## VARIABLES

A variable is a value used by the program that can change. For example, the most recent n-day relative high (a day whose high is higher than the highest high in the prior and succeeding n days) can be represented by the variable Rhigh. The value of Rhigh would change each time a new relative high was defined.

**Format:**

Vars: Variable Name (Initialization value), Variable Name (Initialization value);

Note that variables can be abbreviated as vars.

**Example:**

The following is a sample line for a system that contains three variables, a relative high, a relative low, and a counter:

```
Vars: Counter (0), Rhigh (10000), Rlow(-10000);
```

**Key Points:**

- Variables are assigned an initial value by the program, but this value can change as the program goes through time bar by bar.
- A variable can hold only one value at a time.

### INPUT OR VARIABLE?

- If it is a fixed value (constant) or expression for the entire run of the program, then it is an **input**.
- If the value can change, then it is a **variable**.

# LESSON 14: SYSTEM PROGRAMMING TECHNIQUES — IF-THEN STATEMENTS

## IF-THEN

The If-Then statement is the workhorse of programming. It is possible to construct fairly complex systems using nothing more than variations of If-Then statements. The If-Then statement consists of two parts: (1) an expression that can be evaluated as true or false, (2) an action statement that is executed if the expression is true.

**Format:**

IF {true/false expression} THEN {statement};

**Example:**

In a breakout system, the buy signal—a close above the highest high of the past N days--could be written as follows (Note: EasyLanguage is not case sensitive; capitalization is merely used in our illustrations for emphasis or clarity):

```
IF Close > Highest (High, N)[1] THEN
   Buy at market;
```

The term "Highest (High, N)[1]" requires some explanation. This term is an example of a function. The topic of functions will be covered in Lesson 16. For now, suffice it to say that a function is a calculation or list of calculations that is assigned a name. Functions provide a type of shorthand for commonly used calculations, with the function typically replacing many lines of code with a single expression. For example, the function "Highest" used above will return the highest value for the data type in the first term in parentheses (High in this case) for the number of bars indicated by the second term (N in this case). Thus, the term "Highest (High, N)[1]" will return the highest high during the past N days, where N is a parameter (input) in the system.

Note that "[1]" is added to the term to specify that the calculation is for the N-day period ending on the previous bar. If this suffix had not been added, the function would be evaluated for the N-day period ending in the current bar. In this case, the IF condition could never be true, since today's close could never be greater than the highest high during a period including today.

Assuming daily data, the above If-Then statement will check if today's close is greater than the highest high of the past N days, and if it is, the system will go long at the next opening (assuming the system isn't already long). Note that in EasyLanguage, the term "buy at the market" will result in a long position being implemented on the next opening.

## COMPOUND IF-THEN

The compound If-Then statement combines two or more true/false expressions that need to be evaluated to determine whether the "then" statement is executed. These expressions can be combined using "and" or "or." If "and" is used, both expressions (assuming there are only two) must be true in order for the "then" statement to be executed. If "or" is used as the connecting word, then the "then" statement would be executed if either of the two expressions were true.

**Format:**

IF {true/false expression} AND/OR {true/false expression} THEN {statement};

**Examples:**

```
IF Close > Highest(High , N1)[1] AND Close > Close[N2]
THEN Buy at market;
```

In the above example, the system will go long at the market if today's close is greater than the highest high of the prior N1 days **and** if today's close is greater than the close N2 days ago, where N1 and N2 are parameters (inputs). Note that both expressions must be true in order for a buy to be generated.

```
IF Close > Highest(High , N1 )[1] OR Close > Close[N2]
THEN Exitshort at market;
```

In the above example, the system will liquidate a short position (Exitshort is the EasyLanguage term for liquidating a short position) at the market if today's close is greater than the highest high of the prior N1 days **or** if today's close is greater than the close N2 days ago. Note that the short position will be liquidated if either of the expressions is true.

If both the above If-Then statements were used in the same system, then if both conditions were true, the system would reverse from short to long and if only one of the two conditions were true, the system would merely liquidate an existing short position.

**BLOCK IF-THEN**

In a Block If-Then statement, instead of a single statement being executed if the true/false expression is true, there are two or more statements. The first of these statements is preceded by the word "begin," and the last statement is followed by the word "end." Note that there are semicolons placed after each statement and after the word "end," but not after the word "begin."

**Format:**

IF {true/false expression} THEN BEGIN
    {statement};
    {statement};
    {statement};
END;

**Examples:**

```
IF Close > Highest( High , N1 )[1] THEN BEGIN
   Buy at market;
   SellStop = close - k * AvgTrueRange(N2);
   {AvgTrueRange Function explained later}
   ShortCount = 0;
   {ShortCount counts number of days in short position}
END;
```

In the above example, if the close is greater than the highest high of the prior N1-day period, then three actions are taken:

1. The system goes long at the market.

2. A variable called SellStop is set equal to the closing price minus a multiple of the average daily true range. (The term "AvgTrueRange(N2)" is another example of a function, which will be fully explained in Lesson 16.)

3. ShortCount, which is a variable that counts the number of days the system is in a short position, is reset to 0, since the current short position will be liquidated by the buy signal. Thus, the next time a sell signal is received, ShortCount will be at the correct value (0), as opposed to its value at the time buy signal was received.

Keep in mind that in this and other examples in this lesson, we are only looking at segments of code to illustrate specific points, not the entire code for different systems. Therefore, you should only be concerned about understanding the particular segment and not the entire system, which is not shown. Thus, in the example just provided, the intention was to show a realistic example of a block If-Then statement; the purpose of a variable such a ShortCount and how it might integrate into an overall system are irrelevant. In latter lessons, once we have learned all the basic elements of EasyLanguage, we will provide examples of how they can be combined to write the code for complete systems.

Also note in the above and subsequent examples that comments, which are enclosed in curly brackets, have been added to the code. These comments are intended as either succinct summaries of sections of code or explanations of specific lines.

## NESTED IF-THEN

A nested If-Then is simply an If-Then statement that is contained within another If-Then statement

**Example:**

```
{Breakout system that allows up to N2 positions}

IF Close > Highest( High , N1)[1]   THEN BEGIN
     IF LongTrade < N2 THEN BEGIN
     {pyramid option turned on because of multiple
     position}
          Buy at market;
          LongTrade=LongTrade+1;
     END;
     ShortTrade=0;
END;
```

The above is the buy section code for a simple breakout system that allows multiple positions, up to a maximum of N2. Note that the entire section is a Block If-Then, which itself contains another Block If-Then. In the above example, if the close is greater than the highest high of the prior N1-day period, then the system executes a Block If-Then statement. This inner Block If-Then, which is the Nested If-Then statement, checks whether the number of long positions is less than N2. If it is, then two actions are taken: (1) the system goes long at the market, and (2) the count of the number of long positions, which is contained in the variable LongTrade, is increased by one. After this inner Block If-Then is executed, the outer If-Then Block executes one last statement, which resets the count of short positions to 0.

## IF-THEN-ELSE

In the basic If-Then statement, an action statement is executed if the true/false expression is true. The If-Then-Else statement adds to this an action statement that is executed if the expression is false. In other words, if the expression is true we do one thing, else we do another.

**Format:**

IF {true/false expression} THEN {statement} ELSE {statement};

**Example:**

```
IF Close > Highest(High , N)[1] THEN
   Buy at market
ELSE
   ShortCount  =  ShortCount + 1;
{ShortCount increases by 1 each day position is short and
is used to signal liquidation of position when ShortCount
reaches a specified level. ShortCount is an example of a
counter, which will be discussed later.}
```

In the above example, if the close is greater than the highest high of the prior N days, then the system buys at the market. If this condition is not true, then ShortCount, which is a variable that counts the number of days a short position has been held, is increased by one. Note that a comment has been added to the above section of code explaining the purpose of the variable ShortCount.

## BLOCK IF-THEN-ELSE

The relationship between the Block If-Then-Else and the If-Then-Else is analogous to the relationship between the Block If-Then and the If-Then. In both cases, the block version has two or more statements that are executed pending the evaluation of the true/false expression. In the Block If-Then, there will be multiple statements that are executed if the expression is true. In the Block If-Then-Else, this structure will be supplemented by multiple statements that are executed if the expression is false.

As shown in the format description below, the list of statements that is executed if the expression is true is preceded by the words "then begin," and followed by the word "end." The list of statements that is executed if the expression is false is preceded by the words "else begin," and followed by the word "end." Note that there are semicolons placed after each statement and after the last "end," *but not after the first "end."*

**Format:**

IF {true/false expression} THEN BEGIN
        {statement};
        {statement};
        {statement};
END                             {NOTE: NO Semi-colon ";"}
ELSE BEGIN
        {statement};
        {statement};
        {statement};
END;

**Example:**

```
{Following excerpt from breakout system that exits
automatically N2 days after entry.}

IF Close > Highest(High , N1)[1] and BuyLock=0 THEN BEGIN
{To prevent immediate reentry after time exit: If
previous position liquidated on time exit and there has
not been a new sell signal, BuyLock=1}
        Buy at market;
        ShortCount = 0;
        SellLock=0;
END
ELSE BEGIN

        IF MarketPosition = -1 then
        ShortCount = ShortCount+1;
        IF ShortCount = N2 then BEGIN
                Exitshort at market;
                ShortCount = 0;
                SellLock=1;
                {This prevents automatic reentry without new
buy signal.}
        END;
END;
```

The above example of a Block If-Then-Else statement is excerpted from a system whose rules can be summarized as follows:

The system goes long (and covers short if short) when the close is greater than the highest high of the prior N1 days. The system goes short (and covers long if long) when the close is less than the lowest low of the prior N1 days.
A position is automatically liquidated (without a breakout signal) after it has been held for N2 days.
If a position is liquidated by the time hold rule, as opposed to by a breakout signal, no further breakout signals are taken in the same direction until there is an opposite direction breakout signal. For example, if a short position is liquidated because it has been held for N2 days, no new sell signal (i.e., a close below the lowest low of the prior N1 days) would be taken until there was first a buy signal (i.e., a close above the highest high of the prior N1 days). The reason for this rule is to avoid getting back into a trade shortly after it has been liquidated because the maximum time hold period has been reached.

Note that the above example of a Block If-Then-Else statement represents only the buy section (or equivalently, the phase when the system is short) of the system just summarized. The full code for the system would include an analogous sell section, as well as statement lines for the inputs and variables.

Before explaining the above code, we first define the three variables that are contained in this section:

**BuyLock**—A variable that is set either to 0 or 1. When it is equal to 0, buy signals are taken; when it is equal to 1, buy signals are ignored. BuyLock will be set equal to 1 when a long position is liquidated because it has been held for N2 days (as opposed to being liquidated by a sell signal), in order to prevent getting right back into the trade after a new upside breakout. BuyLock is reset to 0 after a new sell signal is received.

**SellLock**—Analogous to BuyLock, this variable is set either to 0 or 1. When it is equal to 0, sell signals are taken; when it is equal to 1, sell signals are ignored. SellLock will be set equal to 1 when a short position is liquidated because it has been held for N2 days (as opposed to being liquidated by a buy signal), in order to prevent getting right back into the trade after a new downside breakout. SellLock is reset to 0 after a new buy signal is received.

**ShortCount**—This variable counts the number of days a short position has been held. (The system also includes an analogous variable, BuyCount, which is not contained in the above excerpt.)

The first line of code checks for a dual condition: (1) a close greater than the highest high of the past N1 days, and (2) BuyLock = 0 (this condition will be met as long as a long position had not been liquidated because it had been held for N2 days). If both these conditions are true, the first block of statements will be executed:

The system will buy at the market.

ShortCount will be reset to 0, since the current short position will be liquidated by the buy signal and we want ShortCount to equal 0 the next time we get a sell signal. SellLock will be set to 0 because the short position is being liquidated by a buy signal (as opposed to the maximum time hold rule), and we therefore want to allow new sell signals to be taken.

If either of the conditions in the first line of code is not true then the second block of statements will be executed:

If the system is currently short, ShortCount, which counts the number of days a short position has been held, will be increased by one.

If ShortCount is equal to N2, meaning the position has been held for the maximum amount of time allowed, then the following set of statements will be executed:

The short position will be liquidated.

ShortCount will be reset to 0, since the short position is being liquidated and we want ShortCount to equal 0 the next time we get a sell signal.

SellLock will be set equal to 1 to prevent taking any new sell signals. (SellLock will be reset to 0 on the next buy signal.)

# LESSON 15: SYSTEM PROGRAMMING TECHNIQUES — LOOPS

Loops are used when we want to execute the same set of statements a number of times. By using a loop, such a set of statements needs to be written only one time.

## FOR LOOP

The For Loop contains a counter variable, which increases by one (or in the descending format decreases by one) each time the set of statements is executed. The number of times the loop is executed is determined by the beginning and ending values of the counter.

**Format:**

*For ascending CounterVariable:*

FOR {CounterVariable} = {number} TO {number} BEGIN
        {statement};
        {statement};
END;

*For descending CounterVariable:*

FOR {CounterVariable} = {number} DOWNTO {number} BEGIN
        {statement};
        {statement};
END;

**Example:**

An up thrust day is a day whose close is greater than the previous day's high; a down thrust day is a day whose close is less than the previous day's low. In the following example, a For Loop is used to find the number of up thrust and down thrust days during past N1 days:

```
StrongCount = 0;
WeakCount = 0;

FOR Counter = 1 TO N1 BEGIN
   If Close[Counter-1]>High[Counter] Then
      StrongCount= StrongCount + 1;
   If Close[Counter-1] < Low[Counter] Then
      WeakCount = WeakCount + 1;
END;
```

The first time through the loop, the variable Counter is equal to 1. Therefore, the first statement in the loop checks whether today's close (Close[0]) is greater than yesterday's high (High[1]), and if it is, StrongCount, which was set equal to 0 before the For Loop, is increased by one to 1. The next line is analogous for WeakCount, which counts the number of down thrust days. After this last statement in the loop is executed, the counter, which is called Counter in our example, is increased by one to 2, and the program repeats all the statements in the loop.

This time around, the first line checks whether yesterday's close (Close[1]) is greater than the high two days ago (High[2]), and if it is, StrongCount is increased by one to 2. The next line is analogous for WeakCount. Counter is then automatically increased by one to 3 and the statements in the loop are executed again, this time comparing the close of 2 days ago with the high and low of 3 days ago. The loop continues repeating until Counter = N1, at which point the loop is executed for the last time. The values of StrongCount and WeakCount after the loop is completed will indicate the number of up thrust and down thrust days, respectively, within the past N1 days.

## WHILE LOOP

### Key Points

- In a For Loop, the number of repetitions of the loop is known; in a While Loop, the number of repetitions of the loop is not known.
- CAUTION! If the true/false condition in the While Loop is never false, an endless loop results, which means the program will run forever or until you hit Ctrl/Alt/Delete or pull the plug.

**Format:**

```
WHILE {true/false expression} BEGIN
       {statement};
       {statement};
END;
```

**Example:**

A wide-ranging day is a day whose range is equal to some multiple of the average daily true range during a recent past period. In the following example, a While Loop is used to find the high and low for the most recent wide-ranging day:

```
Counter = -1;
Search =1;

WHILE Search=1 and CurrentBar > 200 BEGIN
      Counter = Counter + 1;
      If TrueRange[Counter] > K *
   AvgTrueRange(N)[Counter+1]THEN BEGIN
            Search = 0;
            {If this step missing, endless loop may
result}
            WRDHigh = TrueHigh[Counter];
            WRDLow = TrueLow[Counter];
      END;
      If Counter=200 Then
      Search=0;
      {If this step missing, endless loop may result}
END;
```

Note, the above sample code uses several functions—CurrentBar, TrueRange, AvgTrueRange, TrueHigh, and TrueLow—which return the values implied by their names. Functions, which were briefly introduced in Lesson 14, will be fully discussed in Lesson 16.

Each time a While Loop is completed, the program will return to the start of the loop and check to see if the conditions for repeating the loop are still true. If they are, the loop is repeated; if they are not, the program skips to the first line of code after the loop. The first line of the While Loop indicates that two conditions must be met to run the loop: (1) the variable Search needs to be equal to 1, and (2) the current bar must be greater than 200. Note that in order for the loop to stop repeating endlessly, the program must have some way of eventually setting Search equal to some value other than 1.

The first statement in the loop increases the counter variable, Counter, by one. Since counter was set = -1 before the While Loop, the first time through the loop, this line of code will set Counter = 0. The first time through the loop, since Counter = 0, the next line of code will check whether today's ([0]) true range (the range including any price gap from the previous close) is greater than K times the average true range during the prior N days. If it is, the following set of statements are executed:

1. Search is set equal to 0. This action is necessary to get us out of the loop, since the loop will keep repeating as long as Search = 1. (We no longer want to repeat the loop because we have found the most recent wide-ranging day.)
2. WRDHigh, the variable representing the wide-ranging day high is set equal to today's true high (the higher of today's high and yesterday's close).
3. WRDLow, the variable representing the wide-ranging day low, is set equal to today's true low (the lower of today's low and yesterday's low).

If the true range is not greater than K times the past N-day average daily true range, then the program checks whether Counter is equal to 200, which at this point, of course, it is not.

If Search is still equal to 1, which will be the case if the current day was not a wide-ranging day, the loop repeats. This time, the first statement in the loop will increase Counter from 0 to 1. Therefore, the true range comparison will use yesterday's true range ([1]) versus K times its prior N-day average true range. If yesterday does not fulfill the wide-ranging day condition, the loop will be rerun with Counter = 2, and so on. This process will continue until either a wide-ranging day is found or Counter = 200—events that will result in Search being set equal to 0, thereby ending the loop.

## USING FOR LOOP INSTEAD OF WHILE LOOP

In the above While Loop, if either of the two lines noted by comments were missing, an endless loop would have resulted. Such errors are easy to make, and for this reason it may be desirable to use a For Loop instead of a While Loop wherever possible. The following code, which uses a For Loop, performs exactly the same task as the foregoing While Loop.

**Example:**

```
Counter = -1;

FOR Counter = 0 TO 200 BEGIN
      {Final value set at very high number}
      If TrueRange[Counter] > K *
      AvgTrueRange(N)[Counter+1]Then Begin
      {Same as While Loop expression}
            WRDHigh = TrueHigh[Counter];
         WRDLow = TrueLow[Counter];
         Counter = 200; {This will end loop}
      END;
END;
```

Similar to the While Loop, this For Loop will terminate after Counter = 200 if no wide-ranging day has been found up to that point. Note that there is no need for a statement line increasing Counter by 1 (as was the case in the While Loop), since the For Loop automatically increases the counter variable by 1 each time the loop is repeated. Also, there is no need for a line checking whether Counter = 200, since the For Loop automatically terminates once the upper value of the counter variable is reached. The rest of the code within the loop is the same as in the While Loop with one exception: the line "Search = 0" is replaced with the line "Counter = 200." Counter will be set equal to 200 whenever a wide-ranging day is found in order to terminate the loop.

In summary, in this example, the For Loop is more concise than the While Loop, accomplishes the same task, and doesn't run the risk of an endless loop error.

### BETTER APPROACH USING IF-THEN

An even better approach for finding the most recent wide-ranging day is to use an If-Then statement instead of a loop, an alternative that is both simpler and more efficient. This approach checks for a wide-ranging day on each bar as we move through time, revising the existing values for WRDHigh and WRDLow each time there is a new wide-ranging day. This is much more efficient than looking back each day for the most recent wide-ranging day—an approach that involves enormous duplication.

```
IF  TrueRange > K * AvgTrueRange(N)[ 1] THEN BEGIN
     WRDHigh = TrueHigh;
     WRDLow = TrueLow;
END;
```

These four lines, which were also contained within the lengthier code sections of the While Loop and For Loop, represent the entire code required using the If-Then statement approach.

### ANOTHER WHILE LOOP EXAMPLE

Although in the above example we were able to use an If-Then statement instead of a loop, for many applications such an alternative will not be possible. In the following example, we use a While Loop to find the number of past days needed to get N down closes. This number is represented by the variable SurveyDays. For example, if N = 30 and SurveyDays = 40, the implication is that the recent market has been very weak (because we didn't have to go back many days to get 30 down days). If, on the other hand, SurveyDays = 90, the implication is that the market is very strong. The ratio of SurveyDays to N (or the difference between the two) can be used as a trend indicator or an overbought/oversold indicator.

Note that, in this example, the value sought can't be determined bar by bar as we move through time. Hence, a loop must be used.

```
Counter = -1;
Search =1;
DownCount = 0;

WHILE Search=1 and CurrentBar >200 BEGIN
    Counter = Counter + 1;
    IF Close[Counter] < Close[Counter+1] THEN
        DownCount = DownCount +1;
    IF DownCount = N THEN BEGIN
        SurveyDays = Counter+1;
        {Add 1 because first day is day 0.}
        Search = 0;
        {If this step missing, endless loop may result}
    END;
    IF Counter=200 Then
        Search=0;
    {If this step missing, endless loop may result}
END;
```

Note that the conditions for repeating the While Loop are the same as in the previous While Loop example. The line increasing Counter by 1 and the line checking if Counter = 200 are also the same as in the previous While Loop. Therefore, we will focus on the remaining code.

After Counter is increased by 1, the next line checks whether Close[Counter] is less than Close[Counter+1]. If Counter = 0, as will be the case the first time through the loop, this comparison will be equivalent to checking whether today's close is less than yesterday's close. The next time through the loop, this comparison will be equivalent to checking whether the close of 1 day ago (yesterday) was less than the close of 2 days ago, and so on. If Close[Counter] is less than Close[Counter+1], DownCount, the variable that counts the number of down days, is increased by 1. Then the program checks to see if the count of the number of down days has reached N. If it has, the variable SurveyDays is set equal to Counter + 1 (see comment in code) and Search is set equal to 0 in order to terminate the loop.

## ALTERNATIVE APPROACH USING FOR LOOP

As discussed previously, it may be desirable to use a For Loop instead of a While Loop wherever possible in order to avoid the danger of an endless loop error. The following code, which uses a For Loop, performs exactly the same task as the foregoing While Loop in more concise fashion.

```
Counter = 0;
Search =1;
DownCount = 0;

FOR Counter = 0 TO 200 BEGIN
     IF Close[Counter] < Close[Counter + 1] THEN BEGIN
         DownCount = DownCount + 1;
         IF DownCount = N THEN BEGIN
             SurveyDays = Counter+1;
       {Add 1 because first day is day 0.}
             Counter = 200;
         END;
     END;
END;
```

Similar to the While Loop, this For Loop will terminate after Counter = 200 if DownCount has not reached N by that point. Note that there is no need for a statement line increasing Counter by 1 (as was the case in the While Loop), since the For Loop automatically increases the counter variable by 1 each time the loop is repeated. Also there is no need for a line checking whether Counter = 200, since the For Loop automatically terminates once the upper value of the counter variable is reached. Note that the line "Search = 0" in the While Loop has been replaced with the line "Counter = 200." Just as setting Search = 0 terminates the While Loop, setting Counter = 200 terminates the For Loop. The counter will be set equal to 200 to terminate the loop whenever DownCount reaches N.

Even though the number of loop repetitions is not known, a factor that implies the need for a While Loop instead of a For Loop, once again we see that equivalent code can be written using a For Loop. The For Loop is not only more concise, but more importantly has the advantage of avoiding the danger of an endless loop error.

# LESSON 16: SYSTEM PROGRAMMING TECHNIQUES — ADVANCED TOPICS

## ARRAYS

**Key Point:** A **variable** can hold only one value at a time; an **array** can contain many values.

**Example:** If we were interested only in the most recent relative high, we would use a variable; if we wanted to reference any of the last 10 relative highs, we would use an array. (A relative high is a high that is higher than the highest high in the preceding and succeeding N bars, or days.)

**Format for Declaring an Array:**

Array: ArrayName[Number of elements in array - 1](Initialization Value);

For example: Array: RH[9](0);

In this example, RH is the array name, the number of elements in the array is 10, and all the values are initialized to 0. This example will be more fully detailed in the section below.

If the number indicated in brackets is 9, it means that that the array has been defined for 10 elements. This is true because the first element of the array is considered the "0" position element, the second, the "1$^{st}$" position element, and so on. That is why the formula above indicates that the number in the brackets is equal to one less than the number of elements. All of this is simply intended as an explanation of the formula, but makes little practical difference, since the number of elements in the array definition can be any number equal or larger than the number needed. Use a number that will be larger than the number of elements that might be needed under any circumstances, since if the number of elements referenced by the program exceeds the array definition, an error will result.

The initialization value is the value to which all the elements of the array are originally set. Typically, a 0 is used.

**Example:**

Declare an array to hold the 10 most recent 15-day relative highs and then find these highs.

```
Inputs: n(15);
Variables: Counter(0);
Array: RH[9](0);

IF high[n]>= Highest(H,n)[n+1] and High[n] > Highest(H,n)
THEN BEGIN
      FOR counter = 9 DOWNTO 1 BEGIN
            RH[counter]=RH[counter-1];
      END;
      RH[0]=h[n];
END;
```

We rewrite the first line using the value of n (15 in our example) instead of n, since doing so will help clarify the description:

```
IF high[15]>= Highest(H,15)[16] and  high[15] >
Highest(H,15)  THEN BEGIN
```

The first line checks whether the high of 15 days ago is greater than two values:
1. The highest high during the 15-day period ending 16 days ago (in other words, the 15-day period *preceding* the day 15 days ago), and
2. The highest high during the 15-day period ending today (in other words, the 15-day period *succeeding* the day 15 days ago).

If the high of 15 days ago is higher than both these values, then it meets the definition of a relative high and we execute the statements in the If-Then Block.

First we enter a For Loop in which the counter counts down from 9 to 1. The first time through the loop the relative high in the 9th position (RH[9]) will be set equal to the relative high currently in the 8th position (RH[8]). The next time through the loop, the relative high in the 8th position (RH[8]) will be set equal to the relative high currently in the 7th position (RH[7]), and so on. The last time through the loop (when the counter = 1), the relative high in the 1st position (RH[1]) will be set equal to the relative high currently in the 0 position (RH[0]). (Remember the first element in the array—the most recent relative high in our example—is the 0 position element, not the 1st position element). This last step will leave the 0 position open, and the last statement line will set the 0 position element (RH[0]) equal to the high of 15 days ago.

In effect, each day the code checks whether the high of 15 days ago was a relative high (a 15-day relative high cannot be defined until 15 days later). If it is, each of the prior relative highs will be moved back one slot (e.g., the prior RH[0] would now become (RH[1]) and so on) and the high of 15 days ago would be defined as the most recent relative high (RH[0]).

In the foregoing example, we needed to use an array instead of a variable because we wanted to track more than one value. Thus, if we only wanted to track the value of the most recent relative high, then a variable would have been appropriate. However, if we want to track multiple relative high values, then an array is needed, since a variable can only hold one value at a time. (Of course, we could also have represented each relative high position with a different variable, but this would have been a clumsy approach vis-à-vis using an array.)

## FUNCTIONS DEFINED

- A function is a calculation or list of calculations that is assigned a name.
  **Example:** Highest

- Functions provide a type of shorthand for commonly used calculations.

- The function typically replaces many lines of code with a single expression.

- Functions are extensions of the computer language, where the name of the function represents a given calculation.

- Functions may, require one or more inputs and return a numeric value.
  **Example:** The function "Highest" requires inputting
  a) type of value (e.g., close), and
  b) number of bars.

- **Format:**

    Function Name (Input1, Input 2)

    **Example**:

    ```
    Highest(Close, N)
    ```

- Function inputs are called "arguments"

- Arguments can be any numeric expression or even another function, as in the following example:

    ```
    Highest(RSI(Close,N2), N1)
    ```

- Functions return a numeric value. For example, the function

    ```
    HighC = Highest(Close, N)
    ```

    will set the variable HighC equal to highest close during past N days.

## EASYLANGUAGE FUNCTIONS

EasyLanguage has literally hundreds of functions. These are divided into categories or types. Below we provide a few examples.

### Example 1:

**Type:** EasyLanguage
**Function:** `Average`
**Inputs:** Price, Length
**Returns:** Average price of past "length" bars
**Usage Example:** `LMA = Average( Close, N)`

### Example 2:

**Type:** EasyLanguage
**Function:** `RSI`
**Inputs:** Price, Length
**Returns:** RSI of past "length" bars
**Usage Example:** `RSIvalue = RSI( Close, N)`

### Example 3:

**Type:** Data Information
**Function:** `CurrentBar`
**Inputs:** none
**Returns:** Bar number of current bar
**Usage Example:** `If CurrentBar > 50`

**Example 4:**

> **Type:** Math & Trig
> **Function:** `AbsValue`
> **Inputs:** value
> **Returns:** Absolute value of number
> **Usage Example:** `AbsPriceChange = AbsValue(C - C[1])`

**Example 5:**

> **Type:** Position Information
> **Function:** `MarketPosition`
> **Inputs:** number of positions ago (0 or blank for current)
> **Returns:** 1 (Long), -1 (Short), 0 (Neutral)
> **Usage Example:** `If MarketPosition = 1`

## CREATING YOUR OWN FUNCTION

Even though EasyLanguage contains a vast assortment of functions, there will be times when you will find it convenient to define your own functions. If there is a calculation or set of calculations that you use frequently, but is not represented by an available function, you may find it useful to create your own function. For example, let's say we frequently want to refer to the highs and lows of wide-ranging days. (As the name implies, a wide-ranging day is a day whose true range—i.e., range including price gap—is significantly wider than the average daily true range during a recent period.) In this case, it might be useful to create functions for the wide-ranging day high and wide-ranging day low.

As a specific example, if we wanted a system that would go long if today's close was greater than the high of the most recent wide-ranging day, we could represent this with the following section of code:

```
IF TrueRange > K * AvgTrueRange(N)[1] THEN
   wrdhigh = TrueHigh;
IF close > wrdhigh THEN
   Buy at market;
```

This code is as concise as it is, because it utilizes three built-in functions: TrueRange, AvgTrueRange, and TrueHigh. The function TrueRange returns the true range of the current bar; the function AvgTrueRange returns the average true range for the past N bars; and the function TrueHigh returns the current bar's true high (i.e., the greater of the current bar high or previous bar close). If we had created our own function for the wide-ranging day high called wrdhigh, then the above code could be further simplified to the following simple line:

```
IF close > wrdhigh (N,K) THEN
   Buy at market;
```

Note that the function wrdhigh takes two inputs: N, which is the number of days used to calculate the prior period average daily true range, and K, which is the multiple of the prior average daily true range that is needed to qualify the current day as a wide-ranging day.

How would we create such a function? The first step in creating any function is to choose the following menu selections: File, New, Function. This will bring up a Create Function box, which will require you to give the function a name. Entering a name and hitting OK will bring up a page to write the function.

The wrdhigh function might be written as follows:

```
Inputs: N(numeric), K (numeric);
{Note: In contrast to the code for a system, in writing
the code for a function, it is necessary to define the
input type such as "numeric" or "numeric series" instead
of default value for input (e.g., 30)}

Vars: whigh(0);

IF TrueRange > K * AvgTrueRange(N)[1] THEN
   whigh = TrueHigh;

wrdhigh = whigh;
```

To determine whether a day is a wide-ranging day, we need to measure whether its true range is greater than the average daily true range during a prior period by a given magnitude. This definition requires setting two parameters, or inputs: the number of days used to measure the prior period average true range (N), and the multiple by which today's true range must exceed the prior period average true range (K).

Now, we could hard code these inputs, that is, set them to fixed values. If this method were used, there would be no need for an input statement line, and the input symbols (N,K) in the code would be replaced by numbers (e.g., 30, 2.0). The disadvantage of this approach is that the input values could not be varied. For example, if we wanted to define wide-ranging days to be days whose true range is 3.0 times the prior period average true range, we could not use our function.

Therefore, it is highly desirable to write functions so that they are flexible enough to allow changing the input values. In order to accomplish this, we place the *type* of input value in the parenthesis after the input name as opposed to an actual value, as we do when writing a system. We will focus on to types of input values (other types include True/False and String):

1. **Numeric or NumericSimple**—Either of these terms are used when the value of the input remains constant from the bar. This is the case for both the inputs in our example, since the same number of prior days (N) that would be used to calculate the average true range would be the same at each bar, as would the multiple (K) used for the true range comparison.
2. **NumericSeries**—This would be used when the input is one whose value depends on the specific bar (e.g., a price series). For example, the input statement line for a function that calculates an average would be as follows:

```
Inputs: Price(NumericSeries),Length(NumericSimple);
```

When we use this function in a system the input statement line of the system would define the Price input as a specific series (e.g., Price(Close) or Price(High) ), whereas the Length input would be defined as a specific value (e.g., Length(20) ).

Now, let's examine the code for our function line by line. After the input statement line, there is a comment that succinctly summarizes the foregoing explanation regarding inputs. The next line defines the one variable used in our function: whigh. Then we have an If-Then statement that checks whether the current bar's true range is greater than K times the average true range of the past N bars, and if it is sets the value of whigh equal to the current bar's true high. The last line of code then sets the function equal to whigh. Thus whenever the function is used in a system, or other TradeStation analysis technique (e.g., indicator, ShowMe, PaintBar), it will return the value of the true high of the most recent wide-ranging day. For example, once we have created our own function for wrdhigh, as in the above example, we could set a variable (e.g., value1) equal to the high of the most recent wide-ranging day with the following simple line:

```
Value1 = wrdhigh (N, K );
```

Where K, and N have been defined in the input statement line of the system.

We could create an analogous function, wrdlow, which would return the true low of the most recent wide-ranging day. As a practical illustration of how these new functions might be used, assume we wanted to plot the most recent wide-ranging day highs and lows on a chart. This could be accomplished by creating a ShowMe (menu selections: File, New, ShowMe) with the following code:

```
Inputs: N(20), k(3);

value1= wrdhigh(N,K);
value2= wrdlow(N,K);

plot1 (value1,"wrdhigh");
plot2 (value2,"wrdlow");
```

Note how simple this task becomes once we have created the functions for the wide-ranging day high and low. The entire program consists of nothing more than an input statement line, two lines that set variables equal to the values returned by our function, and then two plot line statements. The plot statement contains two inputs: 1) the numeric value plotted, and 2) the name of the plot. Note that the word "plot" must be followed by a suffix number. If there are two plots, they are labeled plot1 and plot2.

**FIGURE** 16-1 shows this ShowMe applied to the Swiss franc chart with N = 20 and K = 3.0. Note that wide-ranging days are defined based on the true range (the range including the price gap, if any). Once a wide-ranging day is identified, its true high (i.e., the higher of the high and previous close) and true low (the lower of the low and previous close) are plotted until the next wide-ranging day is defined. The higher the value of K, the fewer days that will be identified as wide-ranging days. For example, **Figure** 16-2 illustrates the same chart with K = 4.

## MIRROR IMAGE OF BUY/SELL RULES

Typically, the sell section of the code for a system will have the identical structure as the buy section, with the difference being changes in specific key words. Therefore, rather than write two separate sections of code, it is usually far more efficient to write the buy section, copy and paste it, and then change the appropriate key words for the sell section. To illustrate this methodology consider the following system code, which includes a comment describing the system, an input statement line, a variable statement line, and buy section code, but no sell section code.

```
{Allows up to n2 positions on new breakout signals. Idea
is that good trends will get initiated for n2 positions,
while some whipsaws will only get partially initiated,
thereby mitigating loss. In a sense, each unit added
requires greater confirmation (i.e., n2 breakouts for
n2th unit).}

Inputs: n1(100), n2(3);
Vars: ShortTrade(0),LongTrade(0);

IF Close > Highest(High , N1)[1]   THEN BEGIN
     IF LongTrade < N2 THEN BEGIN
          Buy at market;
          LongTrade=LongTrade+1;
     END;
     ShortTrade=0;
END;
```

Instead of writing the sell section code, we copy and paste the buy section. We then have the following code after the comment line:

```
Inputs: n1(100), n2(3);
Vars: ShortTrade(0), LongTrade(0);

IF Close > Highest(High , N1)[1]   THEN BEGIN
     IF LongTrade < N2 THEN BEGIN
          Buy at market;
          LongTrade=LongTrade+1;
     END;
     ShortTrade=0;
END;

IF Close > Highest(High , N1)[1]   THEN BEGIN
     IF LongTrade < N2 THEN BEGIN
          buy at market;
          LongTrade=LongTrade+1;
     END;
     ShortTrade=0;
END;
```

We then change the keywords in the second duplicate If-Then Block to be appropriate for the sell case. Thus, for example, in the first line "Highest" is changed to "Lowest," and "High" is changed to "Low." In the second line "LongTrade" is changed to "ShortTrade," and so on. At the end of this process, we have the following complete system code shown below:

```
Inputs: n1(100), n2(3);
Vars: ShortTrade(0), LongTrade(0);

IF Close > Highest(High , N1)[1]   THEN BEGIN
      IF LongTrade < N2 THEN BEGIN
            Buy at market;
            LongTrade=LongTrade+1;
      END;
      ShortTrade=0;
END;

IF Close < Lowest(Low , N1)[1]   THEN BEGIN
      IF ShortTrade < N2 THEN BEGIN
            Sell at market;
            ShortTrade=ShortTrade+1;
      END;
      LongTrade=0;
END;
```

## MONITORS (ON/OFF SWITCHES)

Monitors are variables that are set have two settings: on and off, with a value of "1" typically representing on, and a value of "0" representing off. There are two basic applications for monitors:

### A. To Allow an Action

When the monitor variable is set on (1), it allows for a specific action. An example is provided in the BreakoutTimeConfirm. In this system, a buy signal requires a two-step process:

1. **Preliminary Signal**: an upside breakout (i.e., a close above the prior N-day high);
2. **Confirmation Signal**: a close above the breakout day close at any point after at least N2 days have elapsed.

This system is illustrated in **Figure** 16-3, using a 50-day breakout and a 5-day time confirm. In this particular example, the buy signal is confirmed exactly 5 days after the breakout signal because the close on that day is above the close on the breakout day.

The BuyMonitor is turned on (= 1) when a preliminary buy signal occurs. Once the BuyMonitor is turned on, we begin counting N2 days (the value of this count is held in the variable BuyCount). The BuyMonitor is turned off (= 0) when either the buy signal is confirmed or there is a downside breakout (i.e., preliminary sell signal), in which case we no longer want to monitor for a buy signal. The code for the buy section of this system is provided here:

```
{Buy Side Rules}
{If BuyMonitor on, increment BuyCount}

IF BuyMonitor=1 THEN
   BuyCount = BuyCount+1;

{If BuyMonitor is off (=0), turn on on upside breakout
and set BuyPoint}

IF Close > Highest(High , N)[1] and BuyMonitor=0 THEN
BEGIN
   BuyPoint = Close;
      BuyMonitor = 1;
      SellMonitor = 0;
END;

{Turn BuyMonitor off and reset BuyCount on downside
breakout}

        IF Close < Lowest(Low , N)[1] THEN BEGIN
            BuyMonitor = 0;
            BuyCount = 0;
        END;

        {Check for buy condition}

        IF BuyCount >= N2 AND close > BuyPoint THEN BEGIN
            Buy at market;
            BuyMonitor = 0;     {Reset monitors and count}
            SellMonitor = 0;
            BuyCount = 0;
        END;
```

We have divided this code into four sections. Each section is preceded by a comment that briefly summarizes what the following code section does. In the first section, the BuyCount is incremented by 1 if the BuyMonitor is on (=1). (The BuyMonitor will be on after an upside breakout as long as there has not been any intervening confirmation of the buy signal or downside breakout.) In the second section, if the BuyMonitor is off (=0) and there is an upside breakout, then the BuyMonitor is turned on (=1) and the variable BuyPoint is set equal to the close on that day. The third section turns the BuyMonitor off and resets the BuyCount to 0 if there is a downside breakout. The final section checks for confirmation of a buy signal: `BuyCount >= N2 and close > BuyPoint`. If these conditions are met, then a set of statements is executed.

To summarize, in this system, a monitor is used to activate and deactivate the time count that is employed in confirming signals.

### B. To Prevent an Action

A monitor can also be used to avoid an action. An example of this type of application is provided in the BreakoutTimeExitNoR system. This system enters trades on a breakout signal and exits trades either on an opposite direction breakout or after N2 days have elapsed, whichever comes first. In order to avoid the possibility of repeated oscillations between time exits and re-entries, if a trade is exited because of the time rule, we do not allow any signals in the same direction until an opposite direction breakout has occurred. This prevention is accomplished by setting a monitor called BuyLock (SellLock in the sell case) equal to 1. BuyLock will be set equal to 1 when a long position is exited because of the time rule. When BuyLock=1, upside breakouts will be ignored. Thus, in this case, the monitor prevents an action—getting a buy signal. The buy section code for this system is provided below:

```
{Buy Case (Current Position Short)
{Check for buy signal}

   IF Close > Highest(High , N1)[1] AND BuyLock = 0 THEN
   BEGIN
           Buy at market;
      ShortCount = 0;
      {Reset ShortCount so will = 0 on next sell signal}
      SellLock = 0;    {This allows new sell signal}
      END

      {Check for time exit of short position}

ELSE BEGIN
      IF MarketPosition = -1 THEN
      ShortCount = ShortCount + 1;
      IF ShortCount = N2 Then Begin
           Exitshort at market;
      ShortCount = 0;
      {Reset ShortCount so will = 0 on next sell signal}
           SellLock=1;
```

```
            {If short position liquidated on time exit,
            SellLock =1 to prevent reentry until after new buy
            signal}
            END;
END;
```

The entire code shown consists of a single Block If-Then-Else statement. (This is why there is no semicolon after the first "END"). The first section of this statement checks for a buy signal. Note that a buy signal requires both an upside breakout and BuyLock = 0. Also note that after a buy signal is received, SellLock is set equal to 0 to allow new sell signals.

The second section checks for a time exit of a short position. (If we are monitoring for a buy signal, the existing position, if any, would be short.) ShortCount is a variable that counts the number days the system is short. In the first line of this section, if the system is short, ShortCount is incremented by 1. In the next line, we check whether ShortCount has reached N2. If it has, the short position is liquidated, the ShortCount is reset to 0, and SellLock is set equal to 1 (to prevent re-entry of a short position until there has been a new buy signal).

To summarize, in this system, a monitor is used to prevent taking signals when it is turned on (1).

## COUNTERS

### Loop Counters

- This type of counter was detailed in Lesson 15 in the discussion of the For Loop.
- This type of counter is a built-in part of loop—that is, there is no separate code to increase the counter.
- Instead, the counter increases (or decreases) by 1 for every pass of loop until the ending value reached.
- In the For Loop, the counter increases automatically—that is, there are no conditional requirements for increasing the counter.
- An example of a For Loop application would be if we wanted to check each day how many of the past 50 days (ending today) were up days. In this case, the code that checks whether a day was an up day would be executed 50 times, with the counter in the For Loop running from a starting value of 1 to an ending value of 50, as in the following example:

```
UpCount = 0;
FOR Counter = 1 TO 50 BEGIN
```

```
   IF Close[Counter-1] > Close[Counter] Then
      UpCount=UpCount + 1;
END;
```

Note in this example that there is no explicit code for increasing the counter; the incrementation is built into the For Loop. Also note that the counter in the For Loop increases repeatedly during a *single* bar. In other words, the check of how many of the past 50 days were up days, which is accomplished by the complete cycle through the For Loop, is made each day.

**Non-Loop Counters**

- In a non-loop counter, the instruction for increasing the counter is an explicit part of code as opposed to being part of loop.
- In a non-loop counter, the counter is *increased bar by bar* (if specified conditions are met), in contrast to a loop counter, which is increased (or decreased) repeatedly during a *single* bar.
- The non-loop counter is used to trigger action(s) *when* the counter reaches a specified level, in contrast to a loop counter, which is used as a control to repeat a set of actions *until* the counter reaches a specified level.

The non-loop counter is typically activated and deactivated based on specific conditions. (See, for example, the variables BuyCount and ShortCount in the two code illustrations provided in the previous section, *Monitors (On/Off Switches)*.

- If the counter is activated and there are no other conditions, the counter will increase each bar. The BreakoutTimeConfirm system described in the previous section provided an example of this type of nonconditional counter. In this system, the counter was activated on a breakout bar and automatically increased by 1 each bar until a signal was confirmed or an opposite direction breakout occurred.
- Sometimes, additional conditions are required for the counter to increase. In other words, the counter will not automatically increase each bar after it is activated. An example of this type of conditional counter was found in the BreakoutThrustConfrm system described in an earlier lesson. In this system, the confirmation condition for a breakout buy signal was N2 up thrust bars (bars whose close is greater than the prior bar's high) with closes above the breakout level. In this case, the counter does not increase automatically each bar after it is activated; instead, the counter only increases if two conditions are met: (1) close above previous bar's high, and (2) close above close on breakout bar. The code for the BreakoutThrustConfrm will be identical to the code for the

BreakoutTimeConfrm system provided in the previous section, with the exception of the line that controls how the counter is incremented. This line (and an accompanying comment) is provided below:

```
IF BuyMonitor = 1 AND close > BuyPoint AND
Close > High[1] THEN
   BuyCount = BuyCount + 1;
   {Note: for counter to increase, monitor must be on
   AND close must be above BuyPoint AND day must be
   thrust day}
```

For comparison, below we repeat the analogous line for the BreakoutTimeConfrm system, which once the BuyMonitor is turned on (set equal to 1), increases the count each bar without requiring any additional conditions to be met.

```
IF BuyMonitor =1 THEN
   BuyCount  = BuyCount+1;
```

The entire difference between these two systems (in the buy section) boils down to the phrase: "AND close > BuyPoint AND close > high[1]." In other words, the difference relates to whether the counter increases automatically or conditionally once it is activated.

## DEBUGGING

### Error Correction with Verify

Errors are an unavoidable part of programming. The process of finding and correcting errors, which is called debugging, is an essential part of programming. Part of this debugging is performed automatically by the Power Editor. Before a system or other analysis technique can be used in TradeStation, it must be verified by clicking the Verify icon. This error checker will any error it detects, particularly any errors related to syntax. In addition, it can also provide a message explaining the error. For example, if you inadvertently forget to place a semicolon at the end of a statement and hit the Verify icon, the word following the missing semicolon will be highlighted, and the following error message will come up:

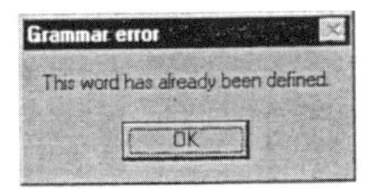

*Grammar error*
*This word has already been defined.*
*OK*

Although this verify feature is excellent in catching errors and providing remedy messages in plain English, the fact that a system verifies successfully does not mean it is error free. Many types of errors, such as logic errors, are not identified in the verify process. Therefore, even if a system verifies successfully you still need to check that it is doing what is intended. Sometimes the fact that something is wrong will be blatantly obvious, as in the example provided in the following section.

**Debugging Example 1**

Assume we want to write a simple breakout system and proceed as follows:

```
{Simple Breakout system}

Input: N(50);

IF Close > Highest(High, N) Then
    Buy at the market;
IF Close < Lowest(Low, N) Then
    Sell at the market;
```

The above system will verify perfectly. However, if you insert the above system into a price chart, any price chart, you will see something odd, or to be more accurate, what you won't see will be odd: you won't see any trading signals. Not one. Why? Look at the above code and see if you can **FIGURE** it out before reading on.

The problem is that we forgot to place a "[1]" after the terms "Highest (High, N)" and "Lowest( Low, N)." Thus, for example, instead of comparing today's close to the highest high of the *prior* 50 days as was intended, we are inadvertently comparing today's close to the highest high of the past 50 days *ending today*. Since it is impossible for today's close to be higher than today's high (it can be equal to today's high, but never higher), there can never be any buy signals. For analogous reasons, there can also never be any sell signals. Therefore, although the above system is perfectly correct, which is why Verify doesn't tag any errors, it is certainly not doing what is intended.

Incidentally, the inadvertent omission of the "[1]" term is one of the most common errors made by novices in EasyLanguage. Keep it in mind. The odds are that sooner or later you will fall for this error as well.

**Using the Expert Commentary for Debugging**

The above system was so simple that finding the error was fairly straightforward. However, in more complex systems, you may not be able to find the source of the error even after carefully reviewing the code. Or, if you are a novice, even the above error may not have been apparent. What do you do then? Fortunately, TradeStation contains a number of tools besides Verify that are great aids in the debugging process. We will illustrate the first of these tools, the Expert Commentary, by showing how it could have been used to find the above error.

First, we need to digress to explain how this tool works and the syntax of the commentary statement (not to be confused with comments) in EasyLanguage. If we click the Expert Commentary icon—an upward-pointing arrow with a capital E—and then click any price bar, a box will come up showing the values of the variables or terms indicated in the commentary statement of the program code.

The general format of the commentary statement is:

```
Commentary ("term1 name", term1, " term2 name", term2, etc.);
```

Note the following points about the syntax of the commentary statement:
- The term name labels and the terms are placed inside of parenthesis following the word "commentary."
- A term can be either a simple variable or a more complex term.
- The name label for each term is placed in quotations.
- A comma separates each part of the commentary statement, names and terms alike.
- It is a good idea to leave extra spaces after each open quotations beginning with the second term name to make sure the screen box will have space between the value of one term and the name of the next term.

To help find the error in the simple breakout system example provided above, we might add the following line of code to the program:

```
Commentary( "Close:", close, "HH:", Highest( High , N));
```

If we add this commentary statement to the system code, click the Expert Commentary icon and then click the price bar of an obvious breakout day, such as January 9, 1998, we see the message box illustrated in **FIGURE** 16-4. We see that even though the close is obviously higher than any high in the prior 50 days, the value shown for the close is less than the value for HH, which is the name label for the term: Highest( High , N). This should alert us that we are not comparing the current bar close to the prior period highest high. With this hint, the omission of "[1]" after the term "Highest( High , N)" may become obvious. We correct the code by adding the suffix "[1]" to the Highest and Lowest function terms, as shown here:

```
IF Close > Highest(High , N)[1] Then
    Buy at the market;
IF Close < Lowest(Low, N)[1] Then
    Sell at the market;
```

After this correction, system signals appear as anticipated (see **Figure** 16-5).

**Debugging Example 2**

**Figure** 16-6 illustrates a 50-day breakout system with the profit target option selected and set to $5,000 (see **Figure** 16-7). Note in **Figure** 16-6 that the system re-enters trades immediately after the position is liquidated on profit objectives being reached. This is obviously not what was intended (even though the first re-entered position makes a large profit in this particular case). In this example, the error is obvious by simply looking at the chart: there is no rule to prevent a new signal from being accepted right after a position has been liquidated on a profit objective. (Debugging by chart is one of the great advantages of TradeStation vis-à-vis standard programming debuggers.) We can correct this problem by modifying the code so that it prevents re-entry until after an opposite direction signal has been received.

Thus the following code for a simple breakout system,

```
Input: N(50);

IF Close > Highest(High, N)[1] THEN
    Buy at the market;
IF Close < Lowest(Low, N)[1] THEN
    Sell at the market;
```

would be replaced with the following:

```
Input: N(50);
Vars: BuyLock(0), SellLock(0);

IF Close > Highest(High, N)[1] and BuyLock=0 THEN BEGIN
    Buy at the market;
    BuyLock=1;
    SellLock=0;
END;

IF Close < Lowest(Low, N)[1] and SellLock=0 THEN BEGIN
    Sell at the market;
    SellLock=1;
```

```
        BuyLock=0;
END;
```

Note that the modified code adds a monitor, BuyLock, that gets set equal to 1 on a buy signal. When BuyLock equals 1, new buy signals are not taken, because the if condition requires BuyLock = 0 in addition to an upside breakout in order to get a buy signal. BuyLock can only get reset to 0 on a sell signal. Thus once a long position is liquidated, a new buy signal cannot occur without an intervening sell signal. Analogous comments would apply in regards to the monitor SellLock, which prevents re-entry of sell signals. **Figure** 16-8 shows the same chart as **Figure** 16-6 with signals based on the modified code. As can be seen, the re-entry signals now disappear, as does the second liquidation signal, since the position was not re-established.

### Debugging Example 3

The following is the code for a breakout system that allows pyramid positions up to a maximum position size of n2 (which is 3 based on the input value):

```
Inputs: n1(50), n2(3);
Vars: ShortTrade(0), LongTrade(0);
IF Close > Highest(High, N1)[1] THEN BEGIN
     IF LongTrade < N2 THEN BEGIN
          Buy at market;
          LongTrade=LongTrade+1;
     END;
     ShortTrade=0;
END;
IF Close <lowest(Low, N1)[1]  THEN BEGIN
     IF ShortTrade < N2 THEN BEGIN
          Sell at market;
          ShortTrade=ShortTrade+1;
     END;
     LongTrade=0;
END;
```

LongTrade keeps track of the number of long positions. As can be seen, upside breakouts will yield buy signals as long as LongTrade is less than N2, which is 3 in this case. Analogous comments would apply to ShortTrade and sell signals. **Figure** 16-9 shows this system applied to the gold market. Although there are repeated downside breakouts after the October 1997 sell signal, no additional sell signals appear. Where are the pyramid units?

In this case, there is nothing wrong with the code. The problem is that the normal setting of the Pyramid Settings section of the Format System/Properties dialog box prohibits multiple positions. In order to allow multiple positions, the "allow multiple entries in same direction by same and different entry signals" button must be selected (see **Figure** 16-10). Once this selection has been made, the anticipated signals appear (see **Figure** 16-11).

**The Data Window and the Print Log**

The Data Window and Print Log are two other TradeStation tools that are useful for debugging. The data window, which can be accessed by the menu selections View, Data Window, or by clicking the "Show/Hide data window" icon, shows the following information for each bar: date, time, open, high, low, close, open interest, and volume. In addition, it will show the values of any indicators plotted on the chart. The limitation of the data window, however, is that it cannot be used to view the values of variable or terms in the code that are not plotted on the chart.

In contrast, the Print Log can be used to view any variable or term in the code, not just line by line, as was the case in the Expert Commentary, but as an entire table. The Print Log can be accessed by the following menu selections: File, New Window, Print Log. In order for data to appear in the Print Log, it is necessary to add a print statement to the code for the system. The format for the print statement is very similar to commentary statement previously discussed. The two are compared below for outputting the values for the same two terms: close and Highest( High , N)[1].

```
Print("Date:", Date:8:0, "Close:", close, "HH:",
Highest(High, N)[1]);

Commentary( "Close:", close,   "HH:",
Highest(High, N)[1]);
```

The one difference is that the commentary statement, which shows data for only one bar at a time, displays the date for the given bar in the screen window; hence no date information is necessary in the commentary statement itself. Since the print statement shows data for all bars in one table, it is necessary to add a date term in the print statement. The syntax for this line is an identifying name label in quotation marks ("Date:" in our example) followed by a comma and the word "Date." The suffix ":8:0" is optional formatting information. The colon after the word "Date" indicates that formatting specifications follow. The number to the left of the second colon indicates the number of spaces to the left of the decimal point; the number to the right of the second colon indicates the number of spaces to the right of the decimal point. This formatting works well for a date. Without this optional formatting information, the date would print with a decimal point and two zeros at the end.

# LESSON 17: CHARTS PATTERNS FOR SYSTEM BUILDING BLOCKS

This section has two purposes:

1. To show how to highlight some key patterns on charts, so that these patterns can be studied for their own sake as a source of trading system ideas.
2. To show how to code a variety of chart patterns. Theses code sections can then be incorporated in system programs that use these patterns.

## GAPS

**Figure** 17-1 shows basic gap up bars in bold. The basic gap up is a bar whose low is higher than the high of the previous bar. The following code is a PaintBar program that colors bars that meet the gap up condition. (For black and white charts, "coloring" would imply using a thicker line weight, as in **Figure** 17-1, which was created using this PaintBar program.) A PaintBar program always requires two plot statements, which together indicate which portion of the bar is to be colored. For example, the code below will color the entire bar from the low to the high. If the second plot statement had used "close" instead of "low," then only the portion of the bar between the close and the high would be colored. Note that each plot statement contains two terms: 1) a point on the bar (e.g., high), and 2) a name in quotations.

```
{Up Gap}

IF low > high[1] THEN BEGIN;
   Plot1(High,"gapup");
   Plot2(Low,"gapup");
END;
```

Basic up and down gaps are rather commonplace. Instead of defining a gap relative to only the previous bar, we may want to define gaps relative to a number of prior bars (multiday gaps), where the number is an input. Thus, if the input value is 5, an up gap would be a bar whose low was greater than the high of the past 5 bars. Thus we need to generalize the gap up program so that it can accommodate any number of prior days in the comparison. All that is required to achieve this generalization is to add an input statement line and to change the term "high[1]" to "highest(high,n1)[1]," as shown below:

```
Inputs: n1(5);

IF low > highest(high,n1)[1] THEN BEGIN;
```

```
  Plot1(High,"gapup");
  Plot2(Low,"gapup");
END;
```

**Figure** 17-2 is the same chart as **Figure**17-1 showing 5-day up gaps instead of the basic 1-day up gaps. Note that by using a 5-day comparison to define gaps, the number of up gaps during the period shown declined from 12 to 3. This section has used upside gaps for illustration; analogous comments would apply to downside gaps.

## ISLAND REVERSALS

A 1-day island reversal is a bar that has a gap relative to both the preceding and succeeding bars. Thus, an island reversal low is a bar whose high is less than the lows of both the previous bar and the following bar. Similarly, an island reversal high is a bar whose low is greater than the highs of both the previous bar and the following bar. Island reversal high and lows are illustrated in **Figure** 17-3.

To make island reversals more meaningful, we require an additional condition that the island reversal high be a significant high and the island reversal low be a significant low. **Figure** 17-4 illustrates 1-day island reversal highs and lows that also met the additional condition of being 50-day highs and lows. These points are marked by large dots. Note there is a relative low on the chart that looks like an island reversal, but is not marked as such because it is not a 1-day island reversal. This issue will be discussed in detail later in this section.

The number of island reversals identified will depend on the value of N, which is the input value that defines how many prior bar highs (or lows) must be exceeded for the point to be identified as an island reversal. **Figure** 17-5 shows the same chart as **Figure** 17-4, with the N value changed from 50 to 5. Note that there are now a number of additional points identified as island reversals.

The following is the code for a ShowMe program that will mark 1-day island reversals, as was done in **Figures** 17-4 and 17-5:

```
Inputs: N(50);

IF low > high[1] AND low[2] > high[1] AND
low[1] < lowest(low,N)[2] Then
    Plot1(low,"IRLow");

IF high < low[1] AND high[2] < low[1] AND
high[1] > highest(high,N)[2] Then
    Plot2(high,"IRHigh");
```

The first If-Then statement will mark the low of a bar that completes the formation (i.e., the day after the gap up) as an island reversal low if three conditions are met:

1. The low is greater than the previous bar's high.
2. The low of 2 bars ago is greater than the previous bar's high.
3. The low of the previous bar was lower than the lowest low of the N-bar period, ending 2 bars ago. (Note the use of "[2]" instead of the typical "[1]" because in this case we are comparing the low of the *previous* bar to the preceding period, as opposed to the low of the *current* bar to the preceding period.)

The second If-Then statement is analogous for marking island reversal highs. As a reminder, the plot statement, which we have encountered before, contains two inputs: 1) the numeric value plotted, and 2) the name of the plot. Also recall that the word "plot" must be followed by a suffix number. If there are two plots, as is the case in this example, they are labeled plot1 and plot2.

Frequently, island reversals are formed only to fail within the following few days. Therefore, it may be useful to add a time confirm to the island reversal pattern. That is, a pattern is not identified as an island reversal low (high) until a specified number of days have passed without that low (high) being penetrated. **Figure** 17-6 is the same chart as **Figure** 17-4, but with only island reversals that have remained intact for at least 5 days being marked. Note that this time confirmation rule eliminates the two false island reversal signals.

The following is the code for the ShowMe program that adds this time confirmation rule:

```
{This program will only identify those 1-day island
reversals whose high/low is not equaled or penetrated
during the next N2 days.}
```

```
Inputs: N(50), N2(5);
Vars: LowMonitor(0), LowPoint (0), LowCount(0);
Vars: HighMonitor(0),HighPoint (0),HighCount(0);

{BOTTOM}
If low > high[1] AND low[2] > high[1] AND
low[1] < lowest(low,N)[2] Then Begin
      LowMonitor = 1;
   {Begin  monitor for time confirm of island reversal}
      LowPoint = Low[1];
   LowCount = -1;
    {Set = -1 so that when incremented in next section
    will equal 0 on day island completed}
End;
If LowMonitor = 1 and low > LowPoint Then Begin
      LowCount = LowCount + 1;
      If LowCount = N2 Then Begin
      plot1[N2](low[N2],"IRLow");
      {Note: both low and plot are offset by N2}
          LowMonitor = 0;
      End;
End;
If LowMonitor = 1 and low <= LowPoint Then
   LowMonitor = 0;

{TOP}
If high <low[1] AND high[2] < low[1] AND
high[1] > highest(high,N)[2] Then Begin
      HighMonitor = 1;
      HighPoint = high[1];
      HighCount = -1;
end;
If HighMonitor = 1 and high < HighPoint Then Begin
      HighCount =HighCount + 1;
      If HighCount = N2 Then Begin
           Plot2[N2](high[N2],"IRHigh");
           HighMonitor = 0;
      End;
End;
If HighMonitor = 1 and high >= HighPoint Then
   HighMonitor = 0;
```

We will focus on the section dealing with an island reversal bottom. Note that when the three conditions for an island reversal bottom are met, instead of marking the day as an island reversal (as was the case in the previous code), the following three actions are taken:

1. LowMonitor, which activates the process of counting days for the time confirm condition, is turned on (set equal to 1).
2. The low of the prior bar is defined as LowPoint. Prices must remain above this point in order for the pattern to be confirmed.
3. LowCount, which counts the number bars for the time confirm condition is set equal to −1. (See comment in code for explanation.)

The next section of code applies only if LowMonitor is on (=1) and the low is greater than the low of the island reversal pattern (LowPoint). If both of these conditions are met, LowCount is incremented by 1. Then the program checks to see whether LowCount has reached N2 (5 in our example). If it has, the island reversal pattern is confirmed and marked and LowMonitor is locked (set equal to 0). Note the comment in the code regarding offset so that the plot occurs at the right point on the chart.

The final line in the "Bottom" section of the code checks to see whether the low is less than LowPoint during the period when LowMonitor = 1. If it is, the island reversal pattern has failed, and we cease monitoring for confirmation of the pattern by setting LowMonitor = 0.

Recall that in **Figure** 17-4 an island reversal bottom was missed because the period between the two gaps exceeded one bar. Ideally, we would like to include such occurrences as island reversals. This more general, or multiday, form of an island reversal bottom would be defined as a gap down bar (whose low is lower than the lowest low of the prior N bars), followed by one or more bars, followed by a gap up bar whose low is higher than the highest high since the gap down bar. (The definition for an island reversal top would be analogous.)

**Figure** 17-7 shows the same price chart as **Figure** 17-4, using this multiday version to identify island reversals. Three multiday reversal bottoms that were not identified in **Figure** 17-4 are now marked. Note that this version of the ShowMe program marks the bar before the first gap (the start of the pattern) and the bar after the second gap (the end of the pattern). **Figure** 17-8 illustrates that island reversal patterns can last for many days, even weeks. The following is the code for the multiday version (which will also encompass 1-day island reversals) of the ShowMe program to mark island reversal bottoms (the program for island reversal tops would be analogous):

```
{Note: This program uses a true/false variable--Flag--
instead of a numeric variable (monitor) set = 0/1.
Exactly equivalent.}

Inputs: N(50);
Vars: Count(0), IHigh(0), Flag(False), GapTop(0);
```

```
{Check for beginning of island bottom--downside gap AND
N-day low}

If high < low[1] and low < Lowest(low,N)[1] then begin
     Count =1;
     GapTop = Low[1];
     IHigh = High;
     Flag = True;
End;

{Check for end of island--upside gap}

If Flag AND Low > IHigh then begin
     Plot2(low,"I_End");
     Plot1[Count](low[Count],"I_Begin");
     Flag = False;
End;

{Check if island maintained--high below top of downside
gap--and update high of island}

If Flag Then Begin
     If High < GapTop Then
          Count = Count +1
     Else
          Flag = False;
     If High > IHigh Then
          IHigh=High;
End;
```

First, note the comment at the start of the program. In this program, we use a true/false variable called Flag. As the name implies, a true/false variable can have one of two values: true or false. This type of variable is entirely equivalent to a numeric variable used as a monitor, which is always set to either 1 or 0. It doesn't make any difference which type of variable is used; it's strictly a matter of preference. We are using the true/false variable here to demonstrate this equivalent alternative to a numeric variable used as a monitor.

This program has four variables:

1. **Count**—A counter variable that keeps track of the number of days since the gap down that started the pattern—information that is needed to appropriately mark the island reversal bottom.

2. **Ihigh**—This variable tracks the high after the gap down—information that will be needed to determine whether a gap up has occurred to complete the formation.
3. **Flag**—A true/false variable that is used just like a monitor. When the variable is true, a number of actions are taken.
4. **GapTop**—This variable is set equal to the top of the first gap. If it is exceeded without a gap up, we stop monitoring for an island reversal bottom.

The first section of the program checks for a gap down, which is also an N-day low—the first event in an island reversal bottom. If a bar fulfills these conditions, the following actions are taken:

1. Count is set equal to 1.
2. GapTop is set equal to the low of the previous bar, which is the top of the gap.
3. Ihigh is set to the high of the bar.
4. Flag is set equal to true.

The next section checks for a gap up—an event that would complete the pattern. If a gap occurs—a low greater than Ihigh, then the beginning and end of the pattern are marked using plot statements. Note that plot1—the mark at the low on the bar preceding the gap down—is offset by Count, as is the low that is plotted. These offsets are indicated by "[Count]" and assure that the correct point is marked. Without this offset, the plot would occur at the point the island reversal is completed. Flag is set to false because the island reversal has now been completed.

The final section checks to see if the island has been maintained—that is, if the high is less than GapTop. If it is, we increase Count by 1. If it isn't, it means the gap has been filled, and we therefore reset Flag to false to stop monitoring for an island reversal bottom. If the gap has not been filled, we also reset Ihigh to the current bar if it is higher than the existing value for Ihigh.

## RELATIVE HIGHS AND LOWS

We have already discussed relative highs in the example for arrays. As a reminder, a relative high is a bar whose high is greater than the preceding or succeeding N bars, where N is an input value. The value of N will greatly affect the number of points that are identified as relative highs or lows. For example, **FIGURE** 17-9 depicts relative highs for the same price chart using two different values of N.

The following is the code for a ShowMe program that will mark relative highs and lows:

```
Inputs: n(10);
```

```
{RELATIVE HIGH}

IF high[n] >= Highest(h,n)[n+1] and
high[n] > Highest(h,n) Then Begin
       Plot1[n](h[n],"RH");
End;

{RELATIVE LOW}

If low[n]<=Lowest(l,n)[n+1] and
low[n]<Lowest(l,n) Then Begin
       Plot2[n] (l[n],"RL");
End;
```

The program begins with an input statement, which declares the input n and initializes it to 10. The If-Then statement that follows checks whether the high n days ago was greater than or equal to the highest high during the preceding and succeeding n days. This same line of code was fully explained in the discussion of arrays in Lesson 16. If you need a further explanation, refer back to that point. If the high of n days ago, or 10 days ago in this example, was greater than or equal to the high of the prior 10 days and greater than the high of the subsequent 10 days, that high is plotted as a relative high.

Note in the plot statement that both the plot and the high are offset by n, or 10, days, because the relative high occurred 10 days ago, not today. In other words, we are plotting the high that occurred 10 days ago, not today's high, and we are marking that point on the bar 10 days ago, not today's bar. This offset is achieved by placing the term "[n]" as a suffix to "plot1" and as a suffix to "h."

The relative low section of code that follows is entirely analogous to the section we have just discussed.

### SPIKES

**FIGURE** 17-10 illustrates spike highs and spike lows. A spike high is a bar whose high exceeds the high of a prior and subsequent number of days by a significant margin, resulting in the bar sticking out like a spike. Similarly, a spike low is a bar whose low is below the low of a prior and subsequent number of days by a significant margin. Spike highs and lows are quite similar to relative highs and lows. Using highs as an example, both the spike high and the relative high exceed the high of a prior and subsequent number of days. The difference is that the spike high must exceed these prior and subsequent highs by a minimum amount. Also, to enhance the likelihood that a spike high is significant, we require it to exceed the high of a minimum number of past days (e.g., 50).

The following is a PaintBar program to color (or thicken) spike high bars:

```
Inputs:  k(0.4),  n(5) ,n2(20), n3(50);

{SPIKE HIGH}

If high[n] >=  Highest(high,n)[n+1] +
(k * AvgTrueRange(n2)) AND high[n] > Highest(high,n) +
(k * AvgTrueRange(n2)) AND high[n] >
Highest(high,n3)[n+1] Then Begin
           Plot1[n] (high[n],"SHH");
           Plot2[n] (low[n],"SHL");
     {Note: [n] necessary to offset to correct bar}
End;
```

There are four inputs:
**k**—a multiple of the average true range by which the spike high must exceed the prior and subsequent period highs;
**n**—the number of past and subsequent days whose high must be exceeded by the specified margin;
**n2**—The number of days used to calculate the average true range;
**n3**—The number of past days whose high must be exceeded by the spike high. The value of n3 will always be greater than n2, usually by a significant margin; otherwise, n3 is a redundant input.

The If-Then statement contains three conditions that must be met. The first two conditions are similar to the conditions that must be met for a relative high, with the exception that the prior and subsequent n-day highs must be exceeded by an amount equal to k * AvgTrueRange(n2). Restating these first two conditions using the input values: the high must exceed the prior and subsequent 5-day highs by an amount equal to or greater than 0.4 times the 20-day average true range. If k were set equal to 0, these first two conditions of the spike high If-Then statement would be identical to the conditions in the If-Then statement for a relative high. The spike high If-Then statement contains a third condition: the high must exceed the high of the past n3 (50) days.

If all three conditions are met the bar is colored. Note, as explained previously, a PaintBar program contains two plot statements, which together describe the portion of the bar that is to be colored. Also note that the plot command and the points plotted are offset by n days for reasons similar to those described in the discussion of relative highs.

## REVERSAL DAYS

The standard definition of a Key Reversal day (low case) is a day with a low below the previous day's low and a close greater than the previous day's close. However, the event described by this definition is so commonplace that it is of little significance and the label "Key Reversal" is a true misnomer. **Figure** 17-11 shows that Key Reversals are about as rare as lobbyists in Washington, D.C.

To make Key Reversals more meaningful, we need to supplement the standard definition with one or more additional constraints. **Figure** 17-12 shows the same price chart as **Figure** 17-11 with the constraint that Key Reversal lows (highs) also be 80-day lows (highs). As can be seen, the addition of this condition greatly reduces the number of days identified as Key Reversals. Nevertheless, even in this instance, there can be a number of premature signals before a major turning point is accurately identified, as was the case in the June 1994 bottom. The January 1995 high, on the other hand, was preceded by only two premature signals.

We can filter signals further by requiring that the close on the Key Reversal day exceed more than one prior close. **Figure** 17-13 shows the same price chart as **Figure** 17-12 with the 80-day high/low requirement supplemented by an additional condition: The close on the Key Reversal day must exceed the prior two closes (as opposed to just the prior close in the standard definition). As can be seen, the signal at the major low in June 1994 is now preceded by only one premature signal. In **Figure** 17-14, which shows the subsequent time period for the same market, the signal at the major January 1995 peak was not preceded by any premature signals. The downside of this approach, however, is that the requirement that the close exceed two prior closes can result in eliminating some major bottom and top signals (see, for example, the May 1995 bottom in **Figure** 17-14).

The following is the code for a ShowMe program that identifies Key Reversal highs (the code for Key Reversal lows would be analogous) incorporating the two modifications just discussed.

```
{Differs from standard key reversal in two ways:
1) Requires a close below 1 or more prior days prices
   (closes or lows)
2) Requires the reversal day to be an N-day high/low.}

Inputs: PastDays(1), N(80), Price(close);
```

```
{Reversal High}

If close < Lowest (Price, PastDays)[1] AND
high > highest (high, N)[1] Then Begin
     plot1(high, "KRH");
End;
```

The comment at the top of the program explains the differences between Key Reversals as defined by this code versus the standard definition. There are three inputs:

**PastDays**—the number of past days prices (e.g., closes) that must be penetrated by the current close as one of the conditions for a Key Reversal (note: setting PastDays = 1 deactivates this constraint);

**N**—the number of prior days whose high must be penetrated as one of the conditions for a Key Reversal high (note: setting N = 1 deactivates this constraint);

**Price**—the type of price (e.g., close, high, low) that must be penetrated by the current close as one of the conditions for a Key Reversal.

The If-Then statement contains two conditions that must be met for a day to be identified as a Key Reversal high:

1. The close must be less than the lowest reference price during the past PastDays days. Given the inputs in the code example, this condition can be restated as the close must be less than the close of the past 1 day. The use of as the input value of 1 for PastDays eliminates the constraint implied by this condition vis-à-vis the standard Key Reversal definition.
2. The high must exceed the highest high of the past N (80) days.

If both conditions are met, the day is identified as a Key Reversal high by the plot statement.

Note that by using an input "Price" instead of close in the first condition of the If-Then statement, we provide the flexibility to change the comparison price. For example, by changing the initialization value of "Price" from close to low, we would change the first condition to being a close below the prior PastDays lows (instead of closes).

## THRUST DAYS

An up thrust day is a day whose close is greater than the previous day's high. A down thrust day is a day whose close is less than the previous day's low. A predominance of up (down) thrust days is indicative of a bull (bear) market. Up and down thrust days are illustrated in **Figure** 17-15. The code for thrust days is extremely simple, with the PaintBar program for up thrust days shown below:

```
If close > high[1] Then Begin
      plot1(high,"TDU");
      plot2(low,"TDU");
End;
```

The If-Then statement simply checks if the close is greater than the previous bar's high, and if it is, the bar is colored. As always, a PaintBar requires two plot statements.

## RUN DAYS

An up run day is a day whose high is greater than the high of the prior N days and whose low is less than the low of the subsequent N days. Similarly, a down run day is a day whose low is less than the low of the prior N days and whose high is greater than the high of the subsequent N days. Note that run days are not defined until N days after their occurrence. Run days are illustrated in **Figure** 17-16. Run days tend to predominate during trends; hence their name. The following is the code for a PaintBar program that colors run days:

```
Inputs: N(5);

If high[N] > Highest(high,N)[N+1] AND
low[N] < Lowest(low,N) Then Begin
   plot1[N](high[N],"RDU");
   plot2[N](low[N],"RDU");
End;
```

There is one input, N. The If-Then statement checks for two conditions:
whether the high N days ago is greater than the highest high during the prior N-day period (ending N+1 days ago);
whether the low N days ago is less than the lowest low during the past N-day period (ending today);

If both of these conditions are true, the day is identified as an up run day and the two plot statements are executed. Note that both the plot command and the high and low are offset by N days. This offset is necessary so that the correct bar is colored, since a run day is not identified until N days after its occurrence.

## WIDE-RANGING DAYS

A wide-ranging day is a day whose true range is significantly wider than the average true range of the recent period. Wide-ranging days that close counter to the direction of a prior protracted trend can sometimes provide an early indication of a major trend reversal. **Figures** 17-17 and 17-18 depict an example of a wide-ranging down day near a peak and a wide-ranging up day near a low for Motorola in two successive time periods. The following is the code for a PaintBar program that colors wide-ranging up days:

```
Inputs: N(30), K(2.5);

If AvgTrueRange(1) > K * AvgTrueRange(N)[1] and
close >= close[1] Then Begin
      plot1(high, "WRD");
      plot2(low,"WRD");
End;
```

This program has two inputs: N, the number of days used to calculate the average true range, and K, the multiple by which a day's true range must exceed the average true range in order to be considered a wide-ranging day. K is by far the more important of these two inputs. The higher the level of K, the fewer the number of days that will be identified as wide-ranging days, but the more significant the price action on those days.

This program looks specifically for wide-ranging days that are up days. An analogous program could be used to identify wide-ranging down days. The reason for distinguishing between wide-ranging days that close higher versus wide-ranging days that close lower is that we may want to color these two events differently.

The If-Then statement checks for two conditions that must be met for the day to be identified as a wide-ranging up day:

Today's true range is greater than the average true range of the past N days.
Today's close is greater than or equal to yesterday's close.

If both of these conditions are met, the two plot statements will color the bar.

Incidentally, don't misread the term "AvgTrueRange(1)" as *"yesterday's* true range." The suffix term is "(1)," not "[1]," and is the input value for the function AvgTrueRange, indicating the number of past days, ending today, for which the average true range is calculated—1 in this case. Thus, the term "AvgTrueRange(1)" is equal to *today's* true range.

## FAILURE SIGNALS

The failure of a signal is itself a signal, and frequently a more reliable signal than the signal itself. For example, a spike is an indication of trend reversal. The failure of a spike—that is the upside penetration of a spike high or the downside penetration of a spike low—is an indication that the trend will continue in the direction of the penetration. Failed spikes are illustrated in **Figure** 17-19. Spikes are shown as thick bars, and the upside penetration of these spikes is denoted by the thick dots. Note that these failure points (i.e., penetration of prior spikes) provided signals for price moves counter to the original spike reversals. The code for a ShowMe program to mark failed spike highs is shown below (failed spike lows would be analogous):

```
Inputs:  k(0.4),   n(5) ,n2(20), n3(50);
Vars: BuyPoint(10000), SellPoint(-10000);

{FAILED SPIKE HIGH}

{This section copied with one modification from SpikeHigh
PaintBar code}

If high[n] >=  Highest(high,n)[n+1] +
( k * AvgTrueRange(n2)) AND high[n] >
Highest(high,n) + (k * AvgTrueRange(n2)) AND

high[n] > Highest(high,n3)[n+1] Then Begin
     BuyPoint = high[N];
{Replaces plot statements in SpikeHigh Code}
End;
{This section added to SpikeHigh code}

If close > BuyPoint Then Begin
     plot1(close,"FSH");
     BuyPoint = 10000;
End;
```

The code above consists of two sections. As noted by the comments in the code, the first section is identical to the code for a spike high with one change: the two plot statements are replaced by the line setting the variable BuyPoint equal to the spike high. The second section is added to the PaintBar program for a spike high. This section consists of an If-Then statement that checks if the close is greater than the spike high (the value contained in the variable BuyPoint). If it is, a plot statement marks the point as confirming a failed spike high, and the variable BuyPoint is reset to an extreme value so that it will be impossible for ensuing closes to exceed BuyPoint (that is, until BuyPoint is set equal to a subsequent spike high).

# LESSON 18: TURNING IDEAS INTO SYSTEMS—TREND-FOLLOWING SYSTEMS AND MODIFICATIONS

In this and the following lesson, we will look at how to code many of the systems we have used for illustrations in earlier lessons. First, we need to discuss two general points:

First bar error problem. The first bar to which a system is applied will often show erroneous signals. There is a simple solution to this problem: As a routine practice, enclose the entire system in an If-Then Block statement, with the if condition being, "If current bar > 1."

Exit of last trade. The TradeStation performance table will not include any open trades. We will often, however, want to include the results of the last trade in the performance statistics. This inclusion will be particularly crucial for long-term trend-following systems where the omission of the last open trade could have a major impact on the performance statistics. To include the last open trade in performance statistics, add following line:

**IncludeSystem: "LastDay";**

The IncludeSystem statement includes another system into the current system. Note that the syntax of this statement requires putting the name of the system to be included in quotations after "IncludeSystem:" LastDay is a system that liquidates the current position if the current bar is the last bar on chart. This system is very simple and is shown below:

```
IF LastBarOnChart Then Begin
     Exitlong on close;
     Exitshort on close;
END;
```

LastBarOnChart is an EasyLanguage function that, as its name implies, returns true if the current bar is the last bar.

### CLOSE COMPARISON SYSTEM (MOMENTUM SYSTEM)

This is a very simple system that goes long if the current close is greater than the close of N days ago and goes short if the current close is less than the close of N days ago. This system is illustrated in **Figure** 18-1 for N=100. The code for this system would be as follows:

```
Inputs: N(100);

If CurrentBar>1 THEN BEGIN
   IF close > close[N] THEN
      Buy at the market;
   IF close< close[N] THEN
      Sell at the market;
END;

IncludeSystem: "LastDay";
```

The core of this system consists of two If-Then statements that check whether the current close is greater than or less than the close N days ago. Note in this example we have enclosed the basic system in an If-Then Block that will avoid applying the system to the first bar. This example also includes the IncludeSystem statement that will assure that the last open trade is included in the performance results. For reasons explained at the start of this lesson, these lines might be included in all systems, and we show them here to demonstrate how they are incorporated into a system. However, to avoid redundancy and clutter, we will not show these lines in subsequent system code examples.

## CROSSOVER MOVING AVERAGE

The crossover moving average system goes long when the short-term moving average crosses above the long-term moving average and goes short when the short-term moving average crosses below the long-term moving average. This system can be written as follows:

```
Input: Length1(10),Length2(100);

IF Average(Close,Length1) > Average(Close,Length2) Then
   Buy at market;
IF Average(Close,Length1) < Average(Close,Length2) Then
   Sell  at market;
```

The first If-Then statement simply checks whether the average close during the past Length1 bars is greater than the average close during the past Length2 bars. If it is, then a buy signal is generated. The second If-Then statement checks for the reverse case for a sell signal. Although the code as written would provide signals every day, remember that the standard setting in the Pyramid Settings section of the Format System dialog box (Properties tab) will prohibit multiple entries in the same direction.

The same system could also be written as follows:

```
Input: Length1(10),Length2(100);

IF Average(Close,Length1) crosses over
Average(Close,Length2) Then
    Buy at market;
IF Average(Close,Length1) crosses below
Average(Close,Length2) Then
    Sell at market;
```

"Crosses over" and "crosses below" are acceptable phrases in EasyLanguage. Although these two code samples appear to be exactly equivalent, they are not. **Figure** 18-1 illustrates the application of the first approach. In this case, a signal will be generated on the first day after MaxBarsBack have elapsed (100 in this case, since that is the length of the maximum bars needed by any calculation in the system). In other words, the signal is generated before the first crossover, because the system is simply checking whether the short-term moving average is above or below the long-term moving average.

**Figure** 18-2 shows the application of the second approach. In this case, because the system code specifically requires a crossover, a signal is not generated until the first crossover, which occurs in early October 1997.

### MOVING AVERAGE CROSSOVER WITH TIME STOP

This is a moving average system with the addition of a stop rule that will liquidate any trade that closes at a loss after N days. **Figure** 18-3 illustrates this system with N = 40. As can be seen, the long position implemented in March 1984 is liquidated because the market closes below the buy signal point after more than 40 days have elapsed. In this illustration, the stop rule allows the long position to be exited at a significantly better point than the subsequent sell signal. The code for this variation of a moving average system is shown below:

```
{Exits any trade that has a loss after N days.
IMPORTANT NOTE: Must use "crosses over and crosses below"
terminology instead of "> and <," since latter
terminology would result in  position being automatically
reentered right after stop is activated.}

Input: Length1(10), Length2(100), N(40);

If Average(Close,Length1) crosses over
Average(Close,Length2) Then
```

```
      Buy at market
Else
   If Average(Close,Length1) crosses below
   Average(Close,Length2) Then
      Sell   at market
{Time stop exit rules follow}
   Else
      If BarsSinceEntry > N AND MarketPosition = 1 AND
      close <   EntryPrice Then
         Exitlong at market
      Else
         If BarsSinceEntry > N AND MarketPosition = -1
      AND close > EntryPrice Then
            Exitshort at market;
```

As noted in the comment at the top of the code, we need to be sure to use the terminology of "crosses over and crosses below" (the second code version we showed for the basic moving average system) instead of "> and <" (the first version), since the latter approach would result in the position being automatically re-entered right after the stop is activated.

We have divided the code into two sections, even though it is all part of an If-Then-Else string of statements. The first section, which generates the moving average signals, duplicates the code for a basic moving average system, and has already been discussed. Therefore, we only need to focus on the second section, which deals with the stop rule. This section has two Else-if statements. The first of these statements checks for three conditions:

At least N bars have elapsed since entry (`BarSinceEntry` is an EasyLanguage, Position Information category, function that returns the value indicated by its name).
The current position is long (`MarketPosition = 1`).
The close is below the entry price (`EntryPrice` is an EasyLanguage, Position Information category, function that returns the value indicated by its name).

If all three conditions are met, the long position is liquidated. The next Else-If statement is analogous for liquidating a short position.

## MOVING AVERAGE CROSSOVER WITH TIME STOP & RE-ENTRY CONDITION

Although the time stop has the beneficial influence of preventing some losses, as was the case in **Figure** 18-3, it can also have an adverse impact by knocking out some winning trades (see, for example, **Figure** 18-4). In fact, missing even one or two very large winning trades could more than offset the loss reduction benefit of the stop rule. Therefore, to avoid missing out on a windfall profit trade, it is worth considering a re-entry rule that will replace a liquidated position on evidence of a resumption of the trend.

This version of a crossover moving average system supplements the previous version (Moving Average Crossover with Time Stop) with a re-entry rule. Specifically, this version will re-enter a liquidated long position on an N2-day breakout. This rule is intended to avoid the possibility of missing major trends. The code for this version is as follows:

```
{Exits any trade that has a loss after N days. Re-enters
on an N2-day breakout.}

Input: Length1(12),Length2(120),N(40),N2(50);

If Average(Close,Length1) crosses over
Average(Close,Length2) Then
    Buy at market;
If Average(Close,Length1) crosses below
Average(Close,Length2) Then
    Sell at market;

{Time stop exit rules follow}
If BarsSinceEntry > N AND MarketPosition = 1 AND
Close < EntryPrice Then
    Exitlong at market;
If BarsSinceEntry > N AND MarketPosition = -1 AND
Close > EntryPrice Then
    Exitshort at market;

{Re-entry conditions follow}
If MarketPosition = 0 AND MarketPosition(1) = 1 AND close
> highest(high,N2)[1] Then
    Buy at market;
If MarketPosition = 0 AND MarketPosition(1)= -1 AND close
<lowest(low,N2)[1] Then
    Sell at market;
```

This system is exactly the same as the previous system with the exception of the last section of code that deals with the re-entry condition. Therefore, we only need to focus on this last section. This section contains two If-Then statements. The first statement checks for three conditions:

1. The current position is neutral.

2. The previous position (MarketPosition(1) ) was long.
3. The close is greater than the highest high during the N2-bar period, ending on the previous bar.

If all three conditions are met, the prior long position is reinstated. The next If-Then statement is analogous for reinstating a short position.

## MOVING AVERAGE CROSSOVER WITH DYNAMIC STOP & RE-ENTRY CONDITION

**Figure** 18-5 repeats an illustration of a crossover moving average system that uses a dynamic stop rule—in this case, a stop that widens and narrows in line with changes in volatility—and also contains a breakout re-entry condition. This system is similar to the previous system in that it uses moving average crossover signals to establish positions and N2-day breakouts to re-enter liquidated positions. The only difference between the two systems is that this system uses a dynamic stop rule instead of a time stop. Therefore, we only need to focus on the code section dealing with the stop rule, and only this section of the system code is reproduced below:

```
{Dynamic stop exit rules follow}

IF MarketPosition = 1 AND close <
highest(high,BarsSinceEntry)-k*AvgTrueRange(adtr)) Then
    Exitlong at market;
IF MarketPosition = -1 AND close >
(lowest(low,BarsSinceEntry) + k*AvgTrueRange(adtr)) Then
    Exitshort at market;
```

The first If-Then statement checks two conditions:

1. The current position is long.
2. The close is less than K times the average true range subtracted from the highest high since the position was entered. ("Adtr" is an input in the system that specifies the number of days used to calculate the average true range.)

If both these conditions are met, the stop is activated and the long position is liquidated. Note this one statement makes use of three functions, which make it possible for all the calculations required by this fairly complex stop rule to be written in less than two lines. This is but one more example of the incredible efficiency of EasyLanguage in programming trading systems. The second statement in the stop exit section is an analogous statement for the stop on short positions.

## BREAKOUT

In this and the remaining sections of this lesson we examine a wide range of variations of the breakout system, beginning with the basic breakout system in this section. The code for the basic breakout system, which is illustrated in **Figure** 18-6, is very simple:

```
{Simple breakout system }

Input: N(80);

If Close > Highest(High, N)[1] Then
    Buy at market;
If Close < Lowest(Low, N )[1] Then
    Sell at market;
```

The entire system consists of an input statement with a single input, an If-Then statement for the buy condition and an If-Then statement for the sell condition. For example, the first If-Then statement indicates that if the close is higher than the highest high during the past N bars, ending the previous bar, then a buy signal occurs.

## BREAKOUT WITH ADTR CONFIRM

This is the first of several variations that adds a confirmation condition to the basic breakout system. In this version, a breakout signal is not taken—that is, the signal is not confirmed—until the price moves beyond the signal price by an amount equal to K times the average true range. **Figure** 18-7 shows signals for the basic breakout system, as well as confirmation thresholds, in the top chart and signals using the confirmation condition (there is only one) in the bottom chart. The market extension beyond the March 1990 breakout signal by an amount equal to 3 times the average true range results in a confirmed buy signal in April 1990. There is no confirmed sell signal in the period shown in the bottom chart because none of the sell signals is followed by a price move below the sell confirmation threshold. The code for this system (buy case only) is:

```
{Breakout system with penetration of k*ADTR required for
signal confirmation}

Input: N(30), k(3);
Vars: BuyPoint(10000), SellPoint(-10000), BuyMonitor(0),
SellMonitor(0);

{BUY CASE}
```

```
{Start monitor for buy signal  and set BuyPoint}

If Close > Highest(High, N )[1] and BuyMonitor=0 Then
Begin
    BuyPoint = close + k*AvgTrueRange(N);
        BuyMonitor=1;
        SellMonitor=0;
End;

{Monitor for buy condition}

If close > BuyPoint Then Begin
        Buy at market;
        BuyPoint= close + 10000;
        BuyMonitor=0;
        SellMonitor=0;
End;
```

The first section of the buy case code monitors for a breakout buy signal and sets the BuyPoint—a variable that is set equal to the price at which the buy signal is confirmed. The If-Then statement in this section checks for two conditions:
close greater than the highest high during the prior N bars;
BuyMonitor = 0 (that is, there has not yet been an upside breakout).

If both these conditions are met, the following actions are taken:

The variable BuyPoint is set equal to the close plus K times the average true range.

The variable BuyMonitor is turned on (set equal to 1).

The variable SellMonitor is reset equal to 0. (This is necessary so that SellPoint can be reset on the next downside breakout.)

The second section monitors for confirmation of a buy signal—that is, a close greater than BuyPoint. If this occurs, the following actions are taken:

A long position is implemented at the market.

BuyPoint is set to a very high value so that it can't be exceeded until it is reset on the next upside breakout.

BuyMonitor is reset to 0.

SellMonitor is reset to 0.

## BREAKOUT WITH TIME CONFIRM

In this version, the confirmation condition is an N2-day wait followed by a close beyond the breakout price. **Figure** 18-8 shows signals for the basic breakout system and the breakout signal prices (horizontal lines) in the top chart and signals using the confirmation condition in the bottom chart. As can be seen, signals are confirmed when prices close beyond the breakout signal 5 or more days after the breakout. The code for this system (buy case only) is:

```
{After breakout signal is received, BuyMonitor is turned
on (= 1). After specified number of days have passed, buy
signal occurs on any close above original breakout point.
}

Input: N(50),N2(5);
Vars: BuyCount(0), SellCount(0), BuyMonitor(0),
SellMonitor(0), BuyPoint(10000), SellPoint(-10000);

{BUY SIDE RULES}
{If BuyMonitor on, increment BuyCount}

If BuyMonitor = 1 Then
   BuyCount  = BuyCount+1;

{If BuyMonitor is off (=0), turn on on upside breakout}

If Close > Highest(High, N )[1] and BuyMonitor=0 Then
Begin
   BuyPoint = close;
      BuyMonitor = 1;
      SellMonitor = 0;
End;

{Turn BuyMonitor off on downside breakout}

If Close < Lowest(Low, N)[1] Then Begin
      BuyMonitor = 0;
      BuyCount = 0;
End;

{Check for buy condition}

If BuyCount >= N2 AND close > BuyPoint Then Begin
      Buy at market;
      BuyMonitor = 0;    {Reset monitors and count}
      SellMonitor = 0;
```

```
        BuyCount = 0;
End;
```

The first statement in the buy case rules checks if the BuyMonitor is on (it will be on after an upside breakout signal), and if it is, increases BuyCount (the variable that counts the number of days after an upside breakout) by 1. If the BuyMonitor is off ( = 0), we check to see if it should be turned on. In other words, we check to see whether there is an upside breakout: a close above the N-day high. If there is an upside breakout, the following actions are performed:

BuyPoint is set equal to close.

BuyMonitor is set equal to 1, which will allow BuyCount to increment.

SellMonitor is reset to 0.

The next section of code checks whether the BuyMonitor should be turned off because of a downside breakout. In other words, if while we are waiting for the time confirmation conditions to be met, the market witnesses a new N-day downside breakout (that is, a sell signal), then we no longer want to monitor for a buy. If there is a downside breakout (i.e., a close below the lowest low of the prior N days), BuyMonitor and BuyCount are both reset to 0. (BuyCount is set to 0 so that it will be equal to 0 the next time we get an upside breakout signal.)

The last section of code checks for confirmation of the buy signal: a close above BuyPoint (i.e., a close greater than the close at the time of the upside breakout signal) anytime after N2 days have elapsed. If the buy signal is confirmed, a buy signal is generated and BuyMonitor, SellMonitor, and BuyCount are all reset to 0.

There are usually many different ways to write any system; some significantly simpler than others. The code below provides a more straightforward way of writing the system just illustrated.

```
{Alternative way of writing system: BreakoutTimeConfirm}

Input: N(50),N2(5);
Vars: Start(100000), BuyPoint(10000) ,SellPoint(-10000);

{BUY SIDE RULES}

{Set BuyPoint and time reference}

If Close > Highest(High, N )[1] AND BuyPoint=10000 Then
Begin
    BuyPoint = close;
     Start = CurrentBar;
```

```
End;

{Cancel BuyPoint on downside breakout}

If Close < Lowest(Low, N)[1] Then
   BuyPoint =10000;

{Check for buy condition}

If CurrentBar >= Start + N2 AND close > BuyPoint Then
Begin
      Buy at market;
      BuyPoint = 10000;
End;
```

Note that this version of the system code contains only three variables. By using the function CurrentBar, this version is able to eliminate the four monitor and count variables, while adding only one new variable: Start (a variable that is set equal to CurrentBar at the time of the breakout signal).

The first section of code in this version checks for two conditions:
1. a close above the highest high during the prior N bars;
2. BuyPoint = 10000 (i.e., BuyPoint has not been already been reset on an upside breakout).

If both conditions are met, BuyPoint is set equal to the close and Start is set equal to the current bar.

The next part of the code checks for a downside breakout, in which case we want to stop monitoring for a buy signal. Thus, if the close is less than the lowest low during the past N bars, BuyPoint is set equal to a value that is out of range (e.g., 10000).

The last section of code checks for a confirmation of the buy signal, which requires two conditions:
at least N2 bars elapsed since breakout signal (CurrentBar >= Start + N2);
close higher than breakout signal price (close > BuyPoint).
If both conditions are met, a buy signal is generated, and BuyPoint is set to a level that is out of range (10000).

Why did we bother showing the previous version of coding this system instead of directly presenting this more concise approach? There are two reasons:
This example was intended to demonstrate the general point that there are usually many different ways to program any system. The implication is that there may often be a simpler approach to programming a given system than one's initial concept.

The first method of coding this system is very similar to the next system we will discuss. Therefore, instead of writing a new program for the next system, we can simply adapt the first code version of this system.

## BREAKOUT WITH THRUST CONFIRM

This breakout system variation uses thrust days to confirm a breakout signal. (Reminder: an up thrust day is a day whose close is greater than the previous day's high.) Specifically, a breakout buy signal is confirmed after there are N2 up thrust days that also fulfill the condition of having higher closes than the breakout day close. This system is illustrated in **Figure** 18-9. The dashed line is the close of the breakout day. Subsequent up thrust days that are also above this line are numbered sequentially. Since N2 is set to 5 in this example the buy signal is confirmed after the fifth up thrust day.

Except for the one If-Then statement that increments the count, the code for this system will be identical to the *first* version of code shown for the previous system. For the Breakout with Time Confirm that line of code read as follows:

```
If BuyMonitor = 1 Then
    BuyCount = BuyCount + 1;
```

In this system, that line is replaced with the line:

```
If BuyMonitor = 1 AND close > BuyPoint AND
close > high[1] Then
    BuyCount = BuyCount + 1;
```

Thus, in this system, instead of automatically increasing each day when BuyMonitor is on (as is the case with the Breakout with Time Confirm system), BuyCount will only increase if two conditions are met:
close is greater than breakout day close;
day is an up thrust day (close > high[1]).

With the exception of this one-line change, the code for the two systems is identical.

## BREAKOUT WITH TIME EXIT & RE-ENTRY

The previous set of systems were variations of breakout systems with confirmation conditions. The next few systems are variations of breakout systems with automatic time exits. This system version enters trades on breakout signals and exits trades automatically after N2 days if there has not been an opposite direction signal during the interim. This system has no restriction regarding re-entry on new breakouts following the liquidation of a trade. The following is the code for this system (buy case only):

```
{Breakout with automatic exit afterN2 days. Allows re-
entries, in contrast to BreakoutTimeExitNoR, which does
not allow re-entry until opposite direction trend signal
received.}

Inputs :N1(40), N2(30);
Vars :LongCount(0), ShortCount(0);

{BUY CASE (Current Position Short)}

{Check for buy signal}

IF Close > Highest(High , N1 )[1] AND MarketPosition < 1
Then Begin
{Second condition to avoid new long signal on day
Exitlong activated.}
     Buy at market;
     ShortCount = 0;
{Reset ShortCount so will = 0 on next sell signal}
End

{Check for exit of short position}

Else Begin
     IF MarketPosition = -1 Then
     ShortCount = ShortCount + 1;
     IF ShortCount = N2 Then Begin
          Exitshort at market;
     ShortCount = 0;
     {Reset ShortCount so will = 0 on next sell signal}
     End;
End;
```

This system has two inputs:
**N1**—the number of days used in the breakout signal.
**N2**—the number of days a position is held if there is no intervening opposite direction signal.

The system also has two variables:
**LongCount**—tracks the number of days a long position has been held.
**ShortCount**—tracks the number of days a short position has been held.

The first section checks for an upside breakout when the current position is neutral or short. If a breakout occurs, a buy signal is generated and ShortCount is reset to 0 so that it will equal 0 on the next sell signal.

The second section checks for the exit of a short position. First, the program checks whether the current position is short. If it is, then ShortCount is incremented by 1. Then the program checks whether ShortCount has reached N2. If it has, the short position is liquidated and ShortCount is reset to 0 so that it will equal 0 on the next sell signal.

## BREAKOUT WITH TIME EXIT & NO RE-ENTRY

This system differs from the previous system by including a rule that prohibits re-entry of a liquidated trade until an opposite signal is received. To prevent re-entry, this system adds BuyLock/SellLock conditions to the previous system. This system is illustrated in **Figure** 18-10 for an 80-day breakout system with a 200-day time exit. Note that after the time exit in February 1995, the system would have repeatedly issued buy signals without the BuyLock rule. The following is the code for this system (buy case only):

```
{Breakout with automatic exit afterN2 days. Also, no
reentry until opposite signal received.}

Inputs :N1(80), N2(200);
Vars :LongCount(0), ShortCount(0), BuyLock(0),
SellLock(0);

{BUY CASE (Current Position Short)}

{Check for buy signal}

IF Close > Highest(High , N1 )[1] AND BuyLock = 0 Then
Begin
      Buy at market;
      ShortCount = 0;
{Reset ShortCount so will = 0 on next sell signal}
      SellLock = 0;    {This allows new sell signal}
End

{Check for time exit of short position}

Else begin
      IF MarketPosition = -1 Then
      ShortCount = ShortCount + 1;
```

```
    IF ShortCount = N2 Then Begin
       Exitshort at market;
       ShortCount = 0;
       {Reset ShortCount so will = 0 on next sell signal}
            SellLock=1;
       {If short position liquidated on time exit,
       SellLock = 1 to prevent reentry until after new
       buy signal}
       End;
End;
```

The first section checks for a buy signal. Note that in addition to a breakout, BuyLock must be equal to 0 in order to generate a buy signal. BuyLock will be set equal to 1 when a long position is liquidated on the time exit rule; in all other circumstances, BuyLock will equal 0. When the close is greater than the highest high of the past N1 bars and BuyLock = 0, the following actions are taken:

A long position is implemented at the market.

ShortCount is reset to 0 so that it will equal 0 on the next sell signal.

SellLock is set equal to 0 to allow new sell signals.

The second section checks for the exit of a short position. First, the program checks whether the current position is short. If it is, then ShortCount is incremented by 1. Then the program checks whether ShortCount has reached N2. If it has, three actions are taken:

1. The short position is liquidated.
2. ShortCount is reset to 0 so that it will equal 0 on the next sell signal.
3. SellLock is set equal to 1 to prevent re-entry of a short position until after a new buy signal has been received.

A comparison of this system with the previous system will reveal that this third condition is the only difference between the two systems in this second section of code.

### BREAKOUT WITH TIME EXIT & RE-ENTRY FILTER

This version of a breakout system with a time exit allows re-entry, but only as long as filter does not prohibit re-entry. The filter prohibits re-entry once "TrdeLock" number of days have elapsed without an intervening breakout in the opposite direction. The following is the code for this system (buy case only):

```
{Breakout with automatic exit afterN2 days. Allows re-
entries as long as "TrdeLock" number of days have not
elapsed without opposite direction trend signal.}

Inputs :N1(40), N2(30), TrdeLock (180) {***};
Vars :LongCount(0), ShortCount(0), BuyFilter(0),
SellFilter(0) {***};

{BUY CASE (Current Position Short).
NOTE: "{***}" denotes line added to system.}

{Increment BuyFilter if not = 0}

If BuyFilter > 0 Then
   BuyFilter = BuyFilter + 1; {***}

{Check for buy signal}
IF Close > Highest(High , N1 )[1] AND
BuyFilter < TrdeLock {***} AND MarketPosition < 1 Then
Begin
      {Last condition to avoid new long signal on day
   Exitlong activated}
      Buy at market;
      If BuyFilter = 0 Then
      BuyFilter = 1; {Start filter count}        {***}
      ShortCount = 0;
   {Reset ShortCount so will = 0 on next sell signal}
      SellFilter = 0;  {***}
   {Reset SellFilter so will = 0 on next sell signal}
End

{Check for exit of short position}
Else Begin
      IF MarketPosition = -1 Then
      ShortCount = ShortCount + 1;
      IF ShortCount = N2 Then Begin
         Exitshort at market;
      ShortCount = 0;
      {Reset ShortCount so will = 0 on next sell signal}
      End;
End;
```

The Breakout Time Exit with Re-entry Filter system is very similar to the Breakout Time Exit with Re-entry system (the second prior system). The only difference is that this system will prohibit re-entry if more than a specified number of days have elapsed without an opposite direction trend signal. So we only focus on the few changes in the code caused by this modification. These changes are denoted with a triple asterisk. As can be seen, there is an additional input: TrdeLock and two additional variables: BuyFilter and SellFilter

Within the buy case section, there are 4 changes: First, we add a line to increment the BuyFilter count when it is > 0, which will be the case whenever there has not been an intervening sell signal after one or more buy signals. Second, an additional condition is specified for a buy signal: BuyFilter < TrdeLock, wherein BuyFilter is a counter and TrdeLock is an input specifying the maximum number of days that can elapse without a short signal before new long trades are prohibited. Third, if the BuyFilter = 0 when there is a new buy signal, then it is set =1. This starts the count for the number of days after a buy signal without an intervening sell signal. Fourth, if there is a buy signal, the SellFilter is reset to 0 so that it will be = 0 on next sell signal. With the exception of these changes, which are marked by triple asterisks, and analogous changes for the sell case, this program is identical to the code for the Breakout Time Exit with Re-entry system.

## BREAKOUT PYRAMID

The next series of systems are breakout systems that incorporate pyramid signals. This version of the breakout system allows for multiple entries on new breakout signals up to a specified maximum position size, which is defined by the parameter or system input, N2. This system is illustrated in **Figure** 18-11 for a 100-day breakout with a maximum position size of 3. The following is the code for this system (buy case only):

```
{BE SURE TO SET RADIO BUTTON TO MULTIPLE ENTRIES IN
PROPERTIES TAB. Allows up to N2 positions on new breakout
signals.}

Inputs: N1(100), N2(3);
Vars: ShortTrade(0), LongTrade(0);

If CurrentBar > 1 Then Begin

{BUY CASE}

IF Close > Highest(High , N1)[1]   Then Begin
      IF LongTrade < N2 Then Begin
           {pyramid option turned off because of multiple
      position}
      Buy at market;
           LongTrade = LongTrade + 1;
```

```
        End;
        ShortTrade = 0;
End;
```

The first point to be stressed, as is indicated in the comment line, is that in order for the system to generate multiple positions, it is necessary to select the multiple entries button in the Format System dialog box (Properties tab). This was detailed in an earlier lesson in our discussion of pyramid strategies.

As can be seen, the system has two inputs: N1, the number of past day highs/lows to be exceeded for a breakout signal, which is set = 100, and N2, the maximum position size, which is set = 3. Now we step through the buy case. As in a simple breakout system, the If statement checks to see if the close is greater than the highest high during the prior N1 days. If it is, in this system, one additional condition must be met before a buy occurs: LongTrade, which is the variable that counts the number of long positions, must be less than N2, the maximum allowed position size. If it is, we buy at the market and set LongTrade = LongTrade +1, since our long position is increasing by 1. Finally, we reset ShortTrade=0, since there is a new buy signal.

## BREAKOUT PYRAMID ON RETRACEMENT

This system establishes the base position on a breakout and pyramid positions on a retracement followed by a resumption of the trend. Pyramid positions require all of the following:

Short-term breakout in opposite direction of base position;
subsequent short-term breakout in same direction of base position;
most recent position profitable;
total position does not equal maximum position indicated by input.

As a reminder of this system, the **Figure** 18-12 shows the heavily notated chart illustrating this system. This chart was discussed in detail in an earlier lesson. The code for this system (buy case only) is shown below:

```
Inputs: L1(100), L2(10), Number(3);
Vars: BuyMonitor(0), SellMonitor(0), LongNum(0),
ShortNum(0), BuyEntry(0), SellEntry(0);

If CurrentBar >1 Then Begin

{MARKETPOSITION = 0 CASE}

{No Position Case--i.e., until first buy or sell signal
is received. This section necessary because buy and sell
sections only apply if MarketPosition = 1 or -1.}
```

```
    If MarketPosition =0 Then Begin
       If close > Highest(high,L1)[1] Then Begin
                Buy at market;
                LongNum=1;
                BuyEntry = close;
            End;
       If close < Lowest(low,L1)[1]  Then Begin
            Sell at market;
                ShortNum=1;
                SellEntry = close;
            End;
    End;

{BUY CASE}
{Base Position Buy Signal}

If close > Highest(high,L1)[1] and MarketPosition = -1
Then Begin
       Buy at market;
    BuyEntry = close;
    {needed because one of pyramid conditions is that
    last position profitable}
       LongNum =1;
       ShortNum = 0;
       SellMonitor = 0;
       BuyMonitor = 0;
End;

{Activate monitor for pyramid buy signals}

If MarketPosition = 1 AND close < Lowest(low,L2)[1] Then
   BuyMonitor = 1;

{Check for Pyramid Buy Signal}

If BuyMonitor=1 AND close > Highest(high,L2)[1] AND
MarketPosition = 1 AND LongNum < Number Then Begin
      If close > BuyEntry Then Begin
           Buy at market;
           BuyEntry = close;
           LongNum = LongNum + 1;
           BuyMonitor = 0;
      End
   Else
      BuyMonitor = 0;
```

```
          {If last position not profitable,
          reset BuyMonitor to 0.}
End;
```

Similar to the previous system, in order for pyramid signals to be generated, the Multiple Entries button in the Format System dialog box (Properties tab) must be selected.

The inputs are: L1, which is the parameter for the base position breakout signal and is set = 100 in this example. L2, which is the parameter for the short-term breakout and is set = 10 in this example, and Number, which is a parameter representing the maximum allowable position size and is set = 3 in this example.

To review the variables for the buy side—the sell side will be analogous—BuyMonitor is turned on, that is set =1, whenever the system is long and there is an opposite direction short-term breakout. When the BuyMonitor is on, we monitor for the second requirement for a pyramid buy signal, namely, a short-term upside breakout. LongNum counts the number of long positions. BuyEntry is set equal to the close at the time of the buy signal so that we can determine if the most recent position is profitable at the time of the next pyramid signal.

In contrast to the systems discussed thus far, which were basically divided into buy case and sell case sections, this system begins with a market position = 0 case. This section is necessary because until the first signal is received, MarketPosition = 0 and the buy and sell sections only apply if MarketPosition = 1 or -1.

The first line of the If MarketPosition = 0 section checks for a buy signal—that is, it checks if the close is greater than the past L1 day high. If it is, we buy at the market. We then set LongNum =1. LongNum keeps count of our long positions. Finally, we set BuyEntry = close. This information will be needed later to determine whether the most recent position is profitable, which is the third of the four requirements for adding a pyramid position. Then an end statement completes the If-Then block. The next If-Then block is analogous for the sell signal case.

The first section of the buy case section checks for a base position buy signal. There are two requirements for a buy signal:
1. the standard upside breakout signal (i.e., close above the highest high during the prior L1 days);
2. current position is short (in the sell case, which is not shown, this requirement will be current position long).

If both conditions are met, the following actions are taken:
1. A buy signal is generated.

2. BuyEntry is set equal to the close. This information is needed because one of the pyramid conditions is that the most recent position is profitable.
3. LongNum is set equal to 1 because there is now one long position.
4. ShortNum is set equal to 0 because by going long we cover the existing short position.
5. BuyMonitor and SellMonitor are set equal to 0 because having just received a base position signal, we are not monitoring for any pyramid signal until a retracement occurs.

The next section consists of a single If-Then statement that checks for the conditions that will activate BuyMonitor, the monitor for pyramid buy signals. This statement will set BuyMonitor equal to 1 if the current position is long and there is a short-term downside breakout (i.e., close below the lowest low of the past L2 days).

The next section checks for a pyramid buy signal, which requires four conditions:
1. BuyMonitor is on (i.e., BuyMonitor = 1);
2. a short-term upside breakout (i.e., close above the highest high of the past L2 days);
3. current position is long;
4. number of long positions is less than Number, the parameter that defines the maximum position size.

If these conditions are met, the program then checks whether the close is greater than BuyEntry, which determines whether the most recent position is profitable (the third of the four requirements for a pyramid signal). If it is, the following actions are taken:
1. A buy signal is generated.
2. BuyEntry is reset to the current close, since subsequent evaluations of whether the most recent position is profitable will now be based on this pyramid position.
3. LongNum is increased by 1 because the long position has increased by 1.
4. BuyMonitor is reset to 0 because we are no longer monitoring for a pyramid buy signal, having just received one. (Monitoring for a pyramid buy signal will be reactivated when there is another short-term downside breakout.)

If the most recent position is not profitable (the Else condition), then instead of the above four actions the BuyMonitor is reset equal to 0.

## BREAKOUT PYRAMID ON RETRACEMENT WITH STOP

This system is the Same as the Breakout Pyramid on Retracement system described in the previous section with the exception that a stop condition is added. This stop condition will liquidate *pyramid* positions if the following two conditions occur:
- short-term breakout in opposite direction;
- close worse than last pyramid unit.

This system is illustrated in **Figure** 18-13. Note that the stop only affects the pyramid units, not the base position. Also, once pyramid units are stopped out, no new pyramid units are implemented until a new base position is established.

Since the change in this system versus the system detailed in the previous section is the addition of a stop rule, we only need to examine the code that deals with this rule; the rest of the system code will be identical to the previous system. This section of code is shown for the current position long case:

```
{Check for stop conditions on pyramid units}

If CurrentContracts >1 Then Begin

{MarketPosition long case}

If MarketPosition = 1 AND close < BuyEntry AND
close < Lowest(low,L2)[1] Then Begin
   Exitlong (CurrentContracts-1) contracts total at
   market;
{Exit all pyramid units}
      LongNum = Number;
{To prevent reentry of pyramid units in same cycle}
      BuyMonitor = 0;
End;
```

This section begins by checking whether there are any pyramid units. CurrrentContracts is an EasyLanguage function (Position Information category) that returns the value implied by its name. If the number of current contracts is greater than 1, then we check whether the stop conditions are met. The section of code shown performs this check for the current position long case (the current position short case would be analogous).

Three conditions must be met for pyramid long positions to be liquidated:
1. The current market position is long.
2. The close is less than BuyEntry. (In other words, the most recent long position is showing a loss.)

3. There is a short-term downside breakout (i.e., the close is less than the lowest low during the prior L2 days).

If these conditions are met, the following actions are taken:

All pyramid long positions, but only pyramid long positions, are liquidated. Note that this action is achieved by using the command "Exitlong *(CurrentContracts-1)* contracts *total* at the market," instead of "Exitlong at the market." If a liquidation command is only intended to apply to part, instead of all, of an existing position, the syntax requires the following two modifications to the Exitlong (Exitshort) command:

The number of contracts (shares) being liquidated is indicated in parenthesis after "Exitlong" (in this case, "CurrentContracts-1" because the base position is not being liquidated);

The word "total" is inserted after the word "contracts" ("shares").

LongNum, the variable that tracks the number of long positions is set equal to Number, the input value for the maximum allowable position size. Why would we set LongNum = Number when the number of long positions is now equal to 1, since the pyramid units have just been liquidated? The reason is that once pyramid unit are liquidated, we do not want to allow new pyramid units to be implemented during the current cycle (that is, we do not want to allow pyramid units until there is a new base position signal). By setting LongNum = Number, we prevent any new pyramid buy signals from occurring.

BuyMonitor is reset to 0, since we are no longer monitoring for any pyramid buy signals.

# LESSON 19: TURNING IDEAS INTO SYSTEMS — STOCK SYSTEM MODIFICATIONS, PATTERN SYSTEMS & COUNTER-TREND SYSTEMS

## STOCK BASED SYSTEM MODIFICATIONS

In this section we explore variations of the breakout system with modifications intended for stock trading application. Since stocks have historically exhibited a long-term, strong uptrend bias, which is not the case for futures markets, and shorting stocks involves complications vis-à-vis buying stocks, we may want to restrict a stock trading system to buy signals only. The following code modifies the simple breakout system so that it generates buy and liquidate signals instead of buy and sell signals:

```
Input: N(100);

If Close > Highest(High, N)[1] Then
    Buy at market;
If Close < Lowest(Low, N)[1] Then
    Exitlong at market;
```

The only change relative to the conventional simple breakout system is that "Sell" is replaced by "Exitlong."

Recall that for stocks, using a fixed share size (e.g., 1 if buy, sell, and liquidate commands do not specify a trade size) can lead to extreme distortions. For reasons that were fully detailed in Lesson 7, in the case of stocks, it makes much more sense to assume a constant dollar size per trade. The code below modifies the standard simple breakout system to trade $1,000 per trade instead of 1 contract/share per trade:

```
Input: N(100);
variables: number(1);

Number =1000/close[1];

If Close > Highest( High , N)[1] Then
    Buy Number shares at market;
If Close < Lowest( Low , N)[1] Then
    Sell Number shares at market;
```

Note that a variable, Number, has been added to the system. This variable will contain the value for the number of shares to be traded on a new signal. Number is set equal to 1,000 divided by the previous close. Therefore, for example, if a stock closed at $10, Number would equal 100, while if a stock closed at $100, Number would equal 10. In effect, this approach would keep the trade size constant at approximately $1,000. ("Approximately" because the transaction price will not necessarily exactly equal the previous closing price.) Note that in this system version, the words "Number shares" have been inserted in the code after "Buy" and "Sell."

Next we combine both of the aforementioned modifications—buy signals only and constant dollar trade size—into a single system. The code for this system version is shown below:

```
Input: N(100);
variables: number(1);

Number=1000/close[1];

If Close > Highest(High, N)[1] Then
    Buy Number shares at market;
If Close < Lowest(Low, N)[1] Then
    Exitlong at market;
```

The only difference between this and the previous system version is that the words "Sell Number" have been replaced by "Exitlong."

In Lesson 12 we demonstrated how trend-following buy signals could be combined with the various stop options (Stops tab of the Format System dialog box) to form a stock trading system. In this type of system, a trend-following signal (e.g., a breakout) is used to enter a long position, and stops are used to exit the long position. Frequently, it may desirable to build in a minimum wait period for re-entry; otherwise the system may end up getting back into a position shortly after it has been liquidated.

**Figure** 19-1 illustrates a buy-only, 50-day breakout system that trades a constant $1,000 per signal, exits on either a 5% money management stop or a 30% profit retracement/40% floor trailing stop, and includes a 50-day wait rule. Note that the system does not generate a buy signal during the period indicated, despite a plethora of upside breakout days, because less than 50 days have elapsed since the liquidation signal.

The next code sample illustrates a stock system that is similar to the previous system in that it generates only buy signals and trades a constant $1,000 per trade, but differs in respect to using stop options instead of a downside breakout to exit trades. Note that the system version illustrated assumes the inclusion of a minimum wait period for re-entering liquidated long positions.

```
{Breakout with following modifications:
1. Longs only
2. Trade size constant at $1,000 instead of fixed number
of contracts
3. No exit on breakout—stop options used for exit
4. No reentry of long position within N2 days of being
stopped out}

Input: N(100), N2(50);
variables: Number(1), Counter(0);

Number = 1000/close[1];

If Close > Highest(High, N)[1] AND Counter > N2 Then
Begin
{Counter assures minimum wait period for re-entry after
position exited}
    Buy Number shares at market;
    Counter=0;
End;

If MarketPosition=0 Then
    Counter = Counter+1;
```

The top of the code contains a comment that succinctly summarizes exactly what this system does. Note that there is an additional input vis-à-vis the previous system: N2, which represents the minimum wait period for re-entering a long position after a liquidation signal. This system also adds a second variable: Counter, which counts the number of days since the last liquidation signal.

This system version requires two conditions for a buy signal:
- an upside breakout (i.e., close higher than highest high during past N days);
- a minimum of N2 days elapsed since the last liquidation signal (i.e., Counter > N2).

If these conditions are met, the system goes long and resets Counter to 0.

The program also contains an If-Then statement that checks whether the current position is neutral. This statement will be true when the stop options in the Format System dialog box have been triggered. If it is true, Counter is incremented by 1 because we want to track the number of days since the position was liquidated.

## PATTERN BASED SYSTEM MODIFICATIONS

In this next section we focus on pattern-based systems. Although trend-following systems are also pattern-based, it will be recalled that the distinction is that the buy and sell signals of these systems do not depend on the direction of the prevailing trend.

### Consecutive Close

This is a very simple system that goes long if there are a specified number of consecutive up closes and short if there are a specified number of down closes. **Figure** 19-2 illustrates this system for an input value of 3. As can be seen, buy signals occur after 3 up closes and sell signals after 3 down closes. The code for this system is very straightforward:

```
Input: N(3);
Vars: ConsecUp(0), ConsecDown(0);

{Buy Case}

If close > close[1] Then
    ConsecUp = ConsecUp + 1
Else
    ConsecUp = 0;
If ConsecUp = N Then
    Buy at market;

{Sell Case}

If close < close[1] Then
    ConsecDown = ConsecDown + 1
Else
    ConsecDown = 0;
If ConsecDown = N Then
    Sell at market;
```

There is one input, N, the number of consecutive closes in given direction needed for a signal, and two variables, ConsecUp and ConsecDown, that count the number of consecutive closes. The entire system consists of an If-Then-Else statement and an If-Then statement for both the buy and sell case. Examining the buy case, the If-Then-Else statement increases ConsecUp by 1 if the close is greater than the prior close and resets ConsecUp to 0 if it is not. This is followed by an If-Then statement that generates a buy signal if ConsecUp equals N. The sell case is analogous

As mentioned throughout this course, there are invariably many possible approaches for programming any given system. The following is another method of coding the identical system:

```
Input: N(3);

IF MRO(Close <= Close[1], N ,1) = -1 Then
   Buy at market;
IF MRO(Close >= Close[1], N, 1) = -1 Then
   Sell at market;
```

This version of the code is even more concise, containing no variables, and consisting of only a single If-Then statement for the buy case and a single If-Then statement for the sell case. This extreme brevity is made possible by the use of the MRO function. MRO, which stands for most recent occurrence, is an EasyLanguage function that returns the number of bars ago that the specified expression was true. The function contains three arguments(inputs):
1. the condition being searched for;
2. the number of prior bars searched;
3. the occurrence of the condition being sought (for example, most recent is equal to 1, second most recent is equal to 2).

If the condition is not found within the specified number of bars, then the function returns a value of $-1$. Thus, the first If-Then statement checks for the most recent occurrence of a close less than or equal to the previous close during the past 3 bars, since N = 3. If the function returns a value of $-1$, it indicates that none of the past 3 bars exhibited a close that was equal or less than the prior close, which obviously implies that all 3 of the past bars must have contained closes that were greater than the prior close. Therefore, if the specified MRO function returns a value of $-1$, it indicates 3 consecutive up closes, which is our buy condition. Analogous comments would apply to the sell case.

**Consecutive Close Reversal**

This system adds a condition to assure that the string of consecutive closes reverses the prior trend. Specifically, this version of the system requires that the day before the first up day in a string of up closes is an N2-day low close. If this condition is met, it implies that the string of consecutive up closes reverses a prior downtrend.

**Figure** 19-3 illustrates this system for input values of N = 3 and N2 = 20. Note that the indicated instance of 3 consecutive up closes does not result in a buy signal because the day before the first up day was not a 20-day low close. **Figure** 19-4 illustrates the same system for the same stock in the immediately ensuing period.

Note that in this case the indicated instance of 3 consecutive down days results in a sell signal, because the day before the first down day was a 20-day high close. Similarly, the indicated string of 3 consecutive up days results in a buy signal, because the day before the first up day was a 20-day low close.

The code for this system is shown below for the buy case:

```
{Adds reversal condition as requirement for signal. For
example, for a buy signal, the day before first up day of
string needs to be an N2-day low close.}

Input: N(3), N2(20);
Vars: ConsecUp(0), ConsecDown(0);

{BUY CASE}

If close > close[1] Then
    ConsecUp = ConsecUp + 1
Else
    ConsecUp = 0;

If ConsecUp=N AND close[N] < Lowest(close, N2)[N+1] Then
    Buy at market;
{Second condition and addition of N2 input are only
changes relative to ConsecClose1 system}
```

This code for this system is very similar to the code for the first coding version of the previous system. In fact, as noted by the comment at the end of the code, the addition of the input N2 and the addition of the second condition in the last statement (close[N] < Lowest(close, N2)[N+1]) are the only changes relative to this previous system. The added condition for a buy signal simply states that the close of N (3) days ago is lower than the lowest close in the N2-day (20-day) period ending in the prior day (i.e., prior to the day N days ago). This condition assures that the market was in a significant downtrend before the string of N (3) consecutive up days.

**Consecutive Close Reversal with Liquidation**

This system adds a liquidation rule to the system in the previous section. Specifically, for a long position, the stop point is the low of the day fulfilling the Lowest (close, N2) condition, which is the day *before* the string of up closes. This version of the system will liquidate the position on the first close worse than the stop point (see **Figure** 19-5). The following is the code for the buy case of this system:

```
{Adds stop liquidation rule to ConsecCloseReversal
system. NOTE: Code written so that stop pegged off period
preceding trade entry and NOT revised each time there is
a new signal in direction of existing trend.}
{Note: Lines added to the system are denoted by {***}}

Input: N(3), N2(20);
Vars: ConsecUp(0), ConsecDown(0),
LongStop(-10000), ShortStop(10000); (***)

{BUY CASE}
{Update ConsecUp count}

If close > close[1] Then
   ConsecUp = ConsecUp + 1
Else
   ConsecUp = 0;

{Check for buy signal and set stop if signal received}
If ConsecUp = N AND C[N] < Lowest(C, N2)[N+1] Then Begin
   If MarketPosition <= 0 Then
      LongStop = Lowest(low, N)[1]; {***}
{If condition to assure that stop is NOT reset each time
buy conditions are met. In other words, stop frozen to
point set when long position established.}
   Buy at market;
End;

{Check for exit of long on stop condition}
If close < LongStop Then
   Exitlong at market; {***}
```

This system is similar to the system described in the preceding section. As the second comment at the top of the code notes, the portions of this code that differ from the code of the previous system are denoted by a triple asterisk. Therefore, we only need to focus on these changes rather than review the entire system code.

The first change is the addition of two variables: LongStop and ShortStop. As their names imply, these variables will contain the stop points for long and short positions.

The first new line is an If-Then statement that applies if the buy conditions are met. This If-Then statement indicates that if the current position is neutral or short, the stop point, LongStop, is set to the lowest low during the N-day period, ending the prior day. This If-Then condition is intended to prevent the stop from being reset every time the buy conditions are met. In other words, the intention of this system is to fix the stop relative to the lowest N-day low *at the time of the buy signal*. We don't want the stop to change if the buy conditions are met again while we are long. If, instead, our intention was for the stop to change each time the buy conditions were met, then we would write the line without the If-Then condition as simply, "LongStop = Lowest(low, N)[1];"

The one other change in the buy section of the code is the addition of an If-Then statement to check for the stop condition being activated. This line states that if the close is less than the stop point (LongStop), then the long position is liquidated.

## GAP SYSTEMS

The first version of a gap system we examine is one that goes long on a multiday up gap—a gap that exceeds the high of at least the past N days (as opposed to 1 day for a conventional gap)—and short on a multiday down gap. Of course, if N is initialized to 1, then this system will generate signals on basic 1-day gaps. This system is illustrated in **Figure** 19-6 for N = 5. Note that the 5-day up and down gaps generate signals, but that the conventional 1-day up and down gaps do not. The following is the code for this system:

```
{Enter on gap that exceeds high/low of at least past N
days (as opposed to 1 day for conventional gap)}

Inputs: N(5);

If low > Highest(high,N)[1] Then
    Buy at market;
If high < Lowest(low,N)[1] Then
    Sell at market;
```

The code for this system is very simple, consisting of an input statement, a single If-Then statement for the buy case, and a single If-Then statement for the sell case. Using the buy case as an example, the If-Then statement indicates that if the low is greater than the highest high of the prior N days (an N-day upside gap), then a buy signal is generated.

Next we look at a variation of this multiday gap system that adds a stop condition. For a long position, the stop is set to the lowest low during the N2-day period prior to the day of the buy signal. For a short position, the stop is set to the highest high during the N2-day period prior to the day of the sell signal. The following is the code for this system:

```
{Adds liquidation (stop) rule to Gap system}
```

```
Inputs: N(5), N2(10);
Vars: LongStop (-10000), ShortStop (10000);

{Buy Case}

If low >Highest(high,N)[1] Then Begin
     Buy at market;
     LongStop = Lowest(low,N2)[1];
End;

{Sell Case}

If high < Lowest(low,N)[1] Then Begin
     Sell at market;
     ShortStop = Highest(high,N2)[1];
End;

{Check for activation of stops}
If close > ShortStop then
   Exitshort at market;
If close < LongStop then
   Exitlong at market;
```

The buy case checks for an N-day up gap. If one occurs, the system goes long and sets the stop to the lowest low during the prior N2 days, ending yesterday. Note that this system allows the stop point to be reset each time the buy conditions reoccur—that is, each time there is a new N-day up gap. This is in contrast to the Consecutive Close Reversal with Liquidation system, which deliberately fixed the stop point at the time of the signal. Consequently, in this system the statements that set the stop points are not preceded by an If-Then condition. (See Consecutive Close Reversal with Liquidation system for comparison.) The sell case is analogous. **Figure** 19-7 provides an example of the stop on a short position being reset on a new downside gap.

The final section checks for the activation of stops. For example, if the close is less than the long position stop point (LongStop), then the long position is liquidated at the market.

### Wide-Ranging Day #1

Next we examine three system variations based on the concept of wide-ranging days. As a reminder, a wide-ranging day is a day whose true range is greater than a specified multiple of the average true range of the prior period. This first version simply goes long on a close above the true high of the most recent wide-ranging day and short on a close below the true low of the most recent wide-ranging day.

This system is illustrated in **Figure** 19-8, with wide-ranging days shown as thick bars. The close above the true high of the late January wide-ranging day results in a buy signal in February. The first close below the low of the true range of a subsequent wide-ranging day does not occur until May, at which point a sell signal is received.

The following is the code for this system:

```
{Buys on close above true high of wide-ranging day}

inputs: N(30), K(2.0);
variables: BuyPoint(10000), SellPoint(-10000);

{Check for buy and sell signals}

If close > BuyPoint Then
    Buy at market;
If close < SellPoint Then
    Sell at market;

{Check if current day is WRD and if it is redefine buy
and sell points}

If AvgTrueRange(1) > K * AvgTrueRange(N)[1] Then Begin
      BuyPoint = TrueHigh;
      SellPoint = TrueLow;
End;

{Note: Check for signals first, because if signal day is
itself a WRD, checking for a WRD first would eliminate
signal.}
```

This system has two inputs: N—the number of days used to calculate the average true range—and K—the multiple of the average true range required to identify a day as a wide-ranging day. There are two variables to hold the trigger levels for buy and sell signals: BuyPoint and SellPoint.

The first section of code checks for buy and sell signals. A buy signal occurs when the close exceeds BuyPoint, which is equal to the true high of the most recent wide-ranging day. Similarly, a sell signal occurs when the close is below SellPoint, which is equal to the true low of the most recent wide-ranging day.

The next section resets BuyPoint and SellPoint each time there is a new wide-ranging day, with BuyPoint being set to the true high and SellPoint to the true low. A comment at the bottom of the code explains that the code checks for signals before it checks for wide-ranging days because if the signal day itself is also a wide-ranging day, checking for a wide-ranging day first would eliminate the signal.

**Wide-Ranging Day #2**

This version of a wide-ranging day system generalizes the previous system by defining a buy signal as a close above the highest high of the N2-day period ending with most recent wide-ranging day. For the case in which N2=1, this system would be identical to the Wide-Ranging Day #1 system.

**Figure** 19-9 illustrates this system for K=2.0 and N2=5. The thick bars are wide-ranging days and the dots are the 5-day highs and lows on those days, which represent the buy and sell points. The close above the upper dot associated with the late January wide-ranging day results in a buy signal in February. The close below the lower dot associated with the early May wide-ranging day results in a sell signal in late May.

```
{Buys on close above highest high of N2-day period ending
with most recent  wide-ranging day}
{Changes relative to the system are denoted by {***}}

inputs: N(25), N2(5){***}, K(2.0);
variables :BuyPoint(10000), SellPoint(-10000);

{Check for buy and sell signals}

If close > BuyPoint Then
    Buy at market;
If close < SellPoint Then
    Sell at market;

{Check if current day is WRD and if it is redefine buy
and sell points}

If AvgTrueRange(1) > K * AvgTrueRange(N)[1] Then Begin
     BuyPoint = Highest(high, N2); {***}
     SellPoint = Lowest(low,N2); {***}
End;
```

```
{Note: Check for signals first, because if signal day is
itself a WRD, checking for a WRD first would eliminate
signal.}
```

This system is very similar to the Wide-Ranging Day #1 system. Therefore, we only need to focus on the few changes rather than review the entire system. Note that this system includes an additional input, N2, which determines the number of prior days (ending in the wide-ranging day) that are used to calculate the buy and sell points. The only other change is in the section that defines the buy and sell points (BuyPoint and SellPoint). For example, instead of being set equal to the true high of the wide-ranging day, BuyPoint is set equal to the highest high during the N2-day period ending in the wide-ranging day.

**Wide-Ranging Day #3**

This system is a little more complex, but try to go through it, because it provides an excellent example of tying in many of the concepts covered in this series. This system buys on a close above the highest true high of a specified number of past wide-ranging days, in contrast to the Wide-Ranging Day #1 system, which uses only the most recent wide-ranging day. The number of wide-ranging days used in this calculation is represented by the input "Num." In a sense, this system is a generalized form of the Wide-Ranging Day #1 system, since if Num is set equal to 1, this system is identical to the Wide-Ranging Day #1 system.

It should be noted that if Num > 2 (and perhaps even 2), the K value in the wide-ranging day calculation should be lower (e.g., 1.5 instead of 2.0) so that there will be more wide-ranging days. Otherwise, it will sometimes require very large price moves to trigger a signal.

This system is illustrated in **Figure** 19-10 for K=1.5 and Num = 4. Once again, wide-ranging days are depicted by thick bars. The late January sell signal occurred because the market closed below the lowest true low of the prior 4 wide-ranging days. This signal was reversed in February when the market closed above the highest true high of the prior 4 wide-ranging days. The system then reversed back to short in May as the market closed below the lowest true low of the prior 4 wide-ranging days.

Note that the February buy signal occurred on a day that was itself a wide-ranging day. The fact that the code for the system checks for buy and sell signals before checking for new wide-ranging days allows a signal to occur on a wide-ranging day. If the order of these sections of code were reversed, then the buy signal would have been delayed (because the close obviously cannot be higher than the true high on the same day).

The following is the code for this system:

```
{Buys on close above highest true high of past "Num"
wide-ranging days.}

Inputs: N(30), K(1.5), Num(4);
Variables :BuyPoint(10000), SellPoint(-10000),
Counter(0);
Arrays: WRDH[9](0), WRDL[9](0);

{Check for buy and sell signals}

If close > BuyPoint Then
    Buy at market;
If close < SellPoint Then
    Sell at market;

{Check if current day is WRD, and if it is, redefine WRD
arrays and buy and sell points}

If AvgTrueRange(1) > K * AvgTrueRange(N)[1] Then Begin

{Redefine WRD high and low arrays}

      FOR Counter = Num-1 DOWNTO 1 Begin
           WRDH[Counter] = WRDH[Counter-1];
           WRDL[Counter] = WRDL[Counter-1];
      End;
      WRDH[0] = TrueHigh;
      WRDL[0] = TrueLow;

      {Redefine buy and sell points}

      BuyPoint = WRDH[0];
      SellPoint = WRDL[0];
      FOR Counter = 1 TO Num-1 Begin
           BuyPoint = MaxList(BuyPoint ,WRDH[Counter]);
           SellPoint = MinList(SellPoint,
WRDL[Counter]);
      End;
End;
```

This system adds another input, Num, the number of prior wide-ranging days whose true high or low must be penetrated to generate a signal. *(Note: **Figure 19-10** and the example detailed in the video assume Num is initialized to 4. This is the input value* *shown in the code above. However, be aware that the code example in the video erroneously shows this input value as 2.)* This system also adds a variable Counter. In addition, this system includes two arrays.

The section that checks for buy and sell signals is the same as the corresponding section in the Wide-Ranging Day #1 system. The check for a wide-ranging day is also the same. However, the actions taken on a wide-ranging day are more involved and are divided into two subsections. The first subsection redefines the wide-ranging day high and low arrays. A For Loop shifts all the elements of the two arrays one position back (e.g., the previous 3$^{rd}$ position element becomes the 4$^{th}$ position element, etc.).

You may wonder why the For Loop begins with Num-1 (3, in this case) instead of Num (4). The reason was explained in the discussion on arrays in Lesson 16. The first element in an array is the "0" position, not the "1" position. Therefore, if there are four elements in an array, they are numbered 0, 1, 2, and 3, not 1, 2, 3, and 4.

In the above code example, the input value for Num is initialized at 4, and therefore the loop begins with the variable Counter equal to 3 (Num −1). The first time through the For Loop, the position 3 element in the wide-ranging day high array (i.e., the 4$^{th}$ prior wide-ranging day high, counting back from the current bar) is set equal to the existing position 2 value (the 3$^{rd}$ prior wide-ranging day high). (Analogous comments apply to the wide-ranging day low values and will not be duplicated in this discussion). The next time through the For Loop, the position 2 element in the wide-ranging day high array is set equal to the existing position 1 value. The third and final time through the For Loop, the position 1 element in the wide-ranging day high array is set equal to the existing position 0 value.

After exiting the For Loop, the program defines the position 0 values for the wide-ranging day high and wide-ranging day low arrays equal to the current bar true high and true low. In effect, if the current bar is a wide-ranging day, the foregoing sequence of steps will shift each of the wide-ranging day high and low values back one slot, leaving the most recent slots (the 0 positions) to be filled by the current bar true high and low.

The next subsection, which applies if the current bar is a wide-ranging day, redefines the buy and sell points (BuyPoint and SellPoint). Initially, BuyPoint is set equal to the current bar high and SellPoint is set equal to the current bar true low. Then the program enters a For Loop. (This loop will only be described for the variable BuyPoint, but analogous comments apply to SellPoint.) The first time through the loop, BuyPoint is set equal to the greater of its current value, which is equal to the current bar true high, or the true high of the previous wide-ranging day (WRDH[1]).

MaxList is an EasyLanguage function (Math & Trig category) that returns the highest value of the values listed. In this example, MaxList will return the value of WRDH[1] if it is higher than the current BuyPoint value. The next time through the loop, BuyPoint is set equal to the greater of its current value, or the true high of the $2^{nd}$ previous wide-ranging day (WRDH[2]), and so on. At the end of this process, BuyPoint will equal the highest true high of the past Num (4) wide-ranging days (including the current bar).

## COUNTER-TREND SYSTEMS

In the final section of this lesson, we explore coding examples for counter-trend systems by working through 5 variations of a moving average band counter-trend approach.

### Moving Average Band Counter-trend #1

Note: This is the same system labeled ADTR Band Counter-trend (Version 1) in Lesson 3.

A moving average band is defined by adding and subtracting a multiple of the average true range from a moving average. For example, if the length of the moving average is 60 and the multiple is 3.0, the upper band would be equal to the 60-day moving average plus 3 times the average true range, and the lower band would be equal to the 60-day moving average minus 3 times the average true range. The system goes short when the high is above the upper band and long when the low is below the lower band (see **Figure** 19-11).

The following is the code for this system:

```
{Buy if low crosses below lower moving average band.}

Inputs :K(3), N(60);
Variables: UB(0), LB(0);

    {Define price bands}

    UB = Average(close, N ) + K * AvgTrueRange(N);
    LB = Average(close, N) - K * AvgTrueRange(N);

    {Check for signals}

    If low crosses below LB Then
    Buy at market;
    If high crosses above UB Then
    Sell at market;
```

This is a very simple system. The first two-line section defines the upper and lower bands. For example, the upper band is defined as the N-day moving average plus K times the N-day average true range. The next two-line section check for buy signals (a low below the lower band) and sell signals (a high above the upper band).

**Moving Average Band Counter-trend #2**

Note: If the parameter K2 (described below) is set equal to 0, this is the same system labeled ADTR Band Counter-trend (Version 2) in Lesson 3.

This system uses two bands—a wider band to enter positions and a narrower band to exit positions. Thus, the system would go short on a high above the upper end of the wider band, liquidate the short position on a low below the lower end of the narrower band, go long on a low below the lower end of the wider band, and liquidate the long position on a high above the upper end of the narrower band.

The code for this system is shown below:

```
{Same as #1, but with a less restrictive condition for
exit}
Inputs: K(6), K2(0), N(60);
Variables: UB(0), LB(0), UB2(0), LB2(0);

{Define entry thresholds}

UB = Average(close, N )+ K * AvgTrueRange(N);
LB = Average(close, N) - K * AvgTrueRange(N);

{Define exit thresholds}

UB2 = Average(close, N )+ K2 * AvgTrueRange(N);
LB2 = Average(close, N) - K2 * AvgTrueRange(N);

{Check for entry signals}

If low crosses below LB Then
    Buy at market;
If high crosses above UB Then
    Sell at market;

{Check for exit signals}

If low crosses below LB2 then
    Exitshort;
If high crosses above UB2 then
```

```
Exitlong;
```

This system adds an input K2 that controls the width of the narrower band. By definition, K2 would always be set lower than K (the input that controls the width of the wider band). The system also adds two variables, UB2 and LB2, to represent the upper and lower end of the narrower band.

The code is divided into four sections. Two of these sections ("Define entry thresholds" and "Check for entry signals") are the core of the Moving Average Band Counter-trend #1 system and have already been discussed. The remaining two sections are analogous to these two sections, using the input and variable names associated with the narrower band, and checking for exits instead of entries.

Note that if K2 is set equal to 0, then both long and short positions would be liquidated on a return to the median line. This special case of the system is illustrated in **Figure** 19-12.

### Moving Average Band Counter-trend #3

Note: There was no counterpart to this version in Lesson 3.

This version of the system contains two modifications that make it more apropos for trading stocks. These two changes address the following factors intrinsic to trading stocks:

There is a strong, long-term uptrend bias in stocks that does not exist in futures.

The assumption of a constant share trade size will greatly understate the influence of trades in earlier years, a point discussed in great detail in Lesson 7.

Reflecting these considerations, there are two differences between this version and the Moving Average Band Counter-trend #1 system:

This system uses a less restrictive condition for a buy signal than a sell signal.

The trade size is assumed to equal a constant $1,000 instead of a fixed number of contracts.

This system is illustrated in **Figure** 19-13. As can be seen, there are two bands. The lower end of the narrow band is used as the threshold for triggering buy signals, while the higher end of the wider band is used as the threshold for triggering sell signals. Consequently, it is easier to get a buy signal than a sell signal. Also note that the trade size varies and represents that number of shares that when multiplied by the prevailing price equals $1,000.

The following is the code for this system:

```
{This version differs from version #1 in two ways:
1) The buy condition is less restrictive than the sell
condition.
2) The number of contracts/shares is adjusted to equal
1000/close.}

Inputs: K(3), K2(6), N(60);
Variables: UB(0), LB(0), Number(1);

{Calculate # shares for trade}

Number=1000/close[1];

{Define price bands}

UB = Average(close, N )+ K2 * AvgTrueRange(N);
LB = Average(close, N) - K * AvgTrueRange(N); .

{Check for signals}

If low crosses below LB Then
    Buy Number shares at market;
If high crosses above UB Then
    Sell Number shares at market;
```

There are only a few changes in this system version vis-à-vis version #1:

An input, K2, which has a higher value than K, is added for the sell side.

A variable, Number, is added to contain the value of the trade size. This trade size formula was discussed at length in Lesson 7.

The formula for the upper band (UB) substitutes K2, which has a higher value, for K.

The words "Number shares" are inserted after the buy and sell commands. This change will result in "Number" shares being bought and sold, as opposed to the 1 share that would be assumed without any further specification. "Number" will equal that amount of shares that when multiplied by the previous close is equal to $1,000.

**Moving Average Band Counter-trend #4**

Note: This is the same system labeled ADTR Band Counter-trend (Version 3) in Lesson 3.

This version of the system is the same as version #1, with the exception that it adds a stop condition—exit long (short) on a close below (above) the N-day low (high). (It also prohibits buying on the day that the stop condition is fulfilled.) This system is illustrated in **Figure** 19-14 for an N value of 125. A long position was liquidated at the various points indicated because the market closed below the prior 125-day low.

The following is the code for this system:

```
{Same as #1, but adds stop condition-exit on N-day low
(also prohibits buying on day that stop condition
fulfilled)}

Inputs: K(3), N(60), Nday(125);
Variables: UB(0), LB(0);

{Define band lines}

UB = Average(close, N )+ K * AvgTrueRange(N);
LB = Average(close, N) - K * AvgTrueRange(N);

{Check for signals}

If Low crosses below LB AND close > Lowest(low, Nday)[1]
{The 2nd condition is to prevent buying on an N-day low
(the stop condition)}
Then
    Buy at market
Else
    If low crosses below LB Then
        Exitshort;

If high crosses above UB AND
close < Highest(high, Nday)[1] Then
    Sell at market
Else
    If high crosses above UB Then
        Exitlong;

{Check for exit of trades}

If close < Lowest(low, Nday)[1] then
    Exitlong at market;
If  close > Highest(high, Nday)[1] then
    Exitshort at market;
```

This system contains an additional input, Nday, which is used to check for the stop condition being met. The value of Nday should be relatively high; otherwise, the

*Jack Schwager's Complete Guide to Designing and Testing Trading Systems* 173

stop condition will frequently be triggered in the vicinity of new signals. The idea of the Nday input is that, although the system takes counter-trend trades, we don't want to stay counter-trend if there is an extreme (e.g., 125-day) breakout.

The "Define band lines" section is the same as in version #1. The check for signals section has been expanded to add a second condition to prevent getting a new signal on the same day the stop is activated. Examining the buy case, a signal requires a low below the lower band *and* a close greater than the lowest low during the prior N-day period (the absence of this second condition would imply the achievement of the stop condition on long positions). An Else condition is added to assure that if the low is less than the lower band, the short position will be liquidated, even if a buy signal is prevented by the current bar's close being below being the prior N-day low (the stop condition on longs). In other words, even if we can't go long, we want to assure that short positions implemented at the upper band are liquidated when prices fall to the lower band.

This version of the system also adds a section for checking for the exit of trades. If the close is below the lowest low during the past N-day period, long positions are liquidated. Similarly, if the close is above the past N-day high, short positions are liquidated.

**Moving Average Band Counter-trend #5**

Note: This is the same system labeled ADTR Band Counter-trend (Version 4) in Lesson 3.

Note in **Figure** 19-14 that there is nothing in that system version that prevents the almost immediate re-entry of positions. For example, there is a sequence of trades caused by the repeated re-entry of a stopped out long position. To avoid such whipsaw phases due to the oscillation between new signal conditions and stop conditions, this system version prohibits a new counter-trend signal if there has been an N-day low(high) within the past "confirm" days.

**Figure** 19-15 shows the same chart as **Figure** 19-14, but with the system modified so that it does not take new buy signals if there was a 125-day low during the past 50 days. Note that the February and March 1991 buy signals are now eliminated.

The following is the code for this system:

```
{Same as #4, but in addition to adding stop, also
prohibits new counter-trend signal if N-day low(high)
within past "confirm" days.}
```

```
Inputs: K(3), N(60), Nday(125), Nconfirm(50);
Variables: UB(0), LB(0), Counter(0), Confirm(0);

{Define band lines}

UB = Average(close, N )+ K * AvgTrueRange(N);
LB = Average(close, N) - K * AvgTrueRange(N);

{Check for buy signal}

If low crosses below LB AND close> Lowest(low, Nday)[1]
Then Begin
      Confirm = 0;
      FOR counter = 1 TO Nconfirm Begin
      If Close[counter]>Lowest(low,Nday)[Counter+1] Then
         Confirm = Confirm + 1;
      {This For Loop checks past Nconfirm days to see if
      any had a low < Nday low ending previous day. If
      it did, Confirm < Nconfirm.}
      End;
      If Confirm = Nconfirm Then
      Buy at market;
End
Else If low crosses below LB then Exitshort;

{Check for sell signal}

If High crosses above UB AND
Close < Highest(high, Nday)[1] Then Begin
      Confirm=0;
      FOR Counter = 1 TO Nconfirm Begin
      If close[Counter]<Highest(high,Nday)[Counter+1]
      Then
         Confirm = Confirm + 1;
      End;
      If Confirm = Nconfirm Then
      Sell at market;
End
Else
   If high crosses above UB Then
      Exitlong;

{Check for exit of trades}

If close < Lowest(low, Nday)[1] Then
   Exitlong at market;
```

```
If close  > Highest(high, Nday)[1] Then
    Exitshort at market;
```

This version adds an input, Nconfirm, and two variables: Counter and Confirm. In order to facilitate the comparison between this system version and version #1, we will focus on the buy case.

Version #1 generated an automatic buy signal if the low crossed below UB and the close was greater than the lowest low during the past N-days. In contrast, given these conditions, this version must first verify that there were no other closes below the prior N-day lows during the past Nconfirm (50) days in order to generate a buy signal. This verification is achieved by a For Loop that checks each of the past Nconfirm (50) to see whether the close was greater than the lowest low during the prior N days. If a given day passes this check, the variable Confirm is incremented by 1. If upon exiting the For Loop, Confirm, which was set equal to 0 immediately prior to the loop, is equal to Nconfirm, it means that each of the past Nconfirm days had a close greater than the lowest low during the prior N days. Or, to put it another way, none of these days had a close below the prior N-day low. Therefore, the buy signal is confirmed. If the buy condition is not confirmed, the Else-If condition will assure that a short position is liquidated if the low is below the lower band.

# LESSON 20: OPTIMIZATION METHODOLOGY

## BASIC PREMISE OF OPTIMIZATION

The basic premise of optimization is that the parameter sets that did best in the past will continue to exhibit superior performance in the future. For example, if we test a list of parameter sets for a moving average system and find that the 20/80 combination did best, the assumption is that the 20/80 combination will continue to be among the best performing parameter sets in the future. Whether this premise is valid is an important question and is, in fact, the subject of the next lesson. In this lesson, however, we focus on the methodology of optimization.

## FOUR CRITERIA FOR DEFINING BEST PERFORMANCE

There are four basic criteria for determining best performance:

1. **Return**—Normally, return should only be viewed in relative (percent) as opposed to absolute (dollar) terms. In other words, the return of a system must be viewed relative to the funds needed to trade the system (not to be confused with margin requirements, which will drastically understate this figure). However, for the purpose of optimizing a single system on a single market, we can make the simplifying assumption that all the parameter sets require the same amount of funds to trade the system, thereby allowing comparisons on the basis of dollar return alone.

2. **Risk**—Risk measures can take on many forms, but predominantly most risk measures fall into two categories: (a) measures of volatility of returns, and (b) measures of drawdowns in equity. Risk measures will be discussed in detail in Lesson 22.

3. **Parameter Stability**—It is not sufficient to find a parameter set that performs well, it is also necessary to ascertain that the parameter set does not reflect a fluke in testing. For example, if we test a range of parameters in a simple breakout system and find that the value $N = 50$ did best, but $N=40$ and $N = 60$ exhibited below-average performance, we wouldn't have a great deal of confidence in the superiority of $N = 50$. On the other hand, if $N = 90$ did well, but not as well as $N=60$, yet parameters on either side (e.g., $N= 70, 80, 100,$ and $110$) also exhibited superior performance, we would have greater confidence in the potential stability in the performance of that parameter.

4. **Time Stability**—Ideally, we want the performance of a system to be reasonably stable over time. For example, a system that does extremely well over a 20-year period, but within that 20-year period experiences a 3-year period with a large

loss, would be less desirable than a lesser performing system that witnessed no more than a modest loss in any year.

The first two of the above factors can also be collapsed into a single measure: return/risk (e.g., return/maximum drawdown, profit factor)

Although return/risk measures are more meaningful, we will use return as the performance criteria to illustrate optimization. There are three reasons for this:

1.  For most people, return comparisons are easier to relate to than return/risk comparisons. Therefore using return instead of return/risk will clarify our exposition of optimization.
2.  For single market tests, it is possible for some parameter set combinations to show up with extremely high return/risk ratios, even though they make far less money. For example, a parameter set that has only 6 trades in 10 years, all of which are profitable but of short duration, would have an infinite profit factor, but would also make relatively little money.
3.  For comparisons within the same system and same market, different criteria results will tend to be highly correlated (e.g., parameters with the best return will also tend to best in terms of return/risk).

For clarity of exposition, we will illustrate the process of optimization for the single market case. However, for portfolios, market-by-market optimization is likely to result in overfitting. Therefore, in practice, it is probably advisable to use portfolio results instead of market-by-market results for optimization.

## OPTIMIZATION: 1 PARAMETER CASE

We will use the simple breakout system to illustrate optimization for the 1-parameter case. **Figure** 20-1 depicts the returns for a simple breakout system applied to the D-mark for the years 1988-1997. Each vertical bar represents the return for a different parameter value, ranging from 10 to 150.

The basic concept is that we want to find the center of the most profitable region of parameter values, not the single best performing parameter. For example, the parameter with the highest return is 20. However, the parameter one position to the left (10) is the only losing parameter tested, and the parameter to the immediate right is the only above-average performing parameter in the region. In contrast, the parameter value 120 has a lower return than parameter value 20, but is in the approximate center of the most profitable region of parameter values. In this sense, based on past performance, 120 would appear to be a better choice than 20.

## OPTIMIZATION: 2 PARAMETER CASE

To illustrate optimization in the two parameter case we use the breakout system with a time exit—positions are entered on a breakout signal and liquidated after a specified number of days have elapsed (assuming there has not been a breakout signal in the opposite direction during the interim). There are two parameters: (a) the number of days used for the breakout, and (b) the number of days the position is held.

Once again, the basic concept is to find the best performing region, not the best performing single parameter set. **Figure** 20-2 shows a matrix of returns for the system applied to the T-bond market during the years 1988-1997. Each cell indicates the return for a specific parameter set. For example, the combination of a 90-day breakout and a time hold of 100 days made $23,438. The best performing parameter sets (those above $35,000) are shown in bold. Although the 45/40 combination is the single best performing parameter set, it is obviously not in the best performing region.

As an aid to finding the center of the most profitable region, we use the "Centered-9" approach. This method replaces the value in each cell with the average of that cell and the 8 surrounding cells. (For cells along the borders, a 3-cell average is used—the given cell and the cells on either side.) **Figure** 20-3 shows these 9-cell (and 3-cell) averages. The parameter set with the highest "Centered-9" value is the 45/120. This parameter set can be thought of as the approximate center of the best performing region. Note in **Figure** 20-2 that this same parameter set, which is bordered, has a significantly lower return than the 45/40 combination. However, the 45/40 combination, while it is itself the single most profitable parameter set, is surrounded by substantially lower return parameter sets. Therefore, the 45/120 parameter set is far more representative of the optimal region of parameter space (based on past performance).

## OPTIMIZATION: 3 PARAMETER CASE COLLAPSING INTO 2

What do we do when there are 3 parameters, which can no longer be represented in two dimensions? The simplest solution in situations where it is possible is to collapse the three parameters into two. For example, assume a crossover moving average system with a time delay entry. We can assume a fixed ratio between the short-term and long-term moving averages. An example is provided in **Figure** 20-4. Once the value of one moving average is specified, the other is predetermined. Therefore, we only need a single parameter (either the long-term moving average or the short-term moving average) to represent both. We could then apply the 2-parameter case optimization methodology.

What if we wanted to allow for different ratios between the short-term and long-term moving averages, seemingly forcing the need for a third parameter? In this case, the short-term moving average could be fixed and the long-term moving average and ratio could be linked (see **Figure** 20-5). Thus, once the value of the ratio is specified, the value of the long-term moving average would be predetermined. Therefore, in this case, the long-term moving average and ratio could be represented by a single parameter, thereby again allowing us to apply the 2-parameter case optimization methodology.

## OPTIMIZATION: 3 PARAMETER CASE

What if we have a 3 parameter system that does not lend itself to linking two of the parameters? In this case, we could use the following step-by step procedure:

Select the two primary parameters.

For each value of parameter 3, find the highest "Centered-9" value using a matrix based on the two primary parameters.

Chose the value of parameter 3 that has the highest "Centered-9" value.

## OPTIMIZATION FOR > 3 PARAMETER CASE

If there are four parameters, we could repeat the previous process for the selected fixed value of parameter 3 and then vary parameter 4. This approach will not necessarily yield the optimal combination because of interaction between parameters. Obviously this methodology gets a bit unwieldy once you get past 3 parameters. (Note to mathematically inclined viewers/readers: Theoretically, the precise answer could be found using a multidimensional center of mass calculation.) However, in practical terms, it is not necessary to find the single optimal parameter set or to use very sophisticated complex optimization procedures for reasons that are explained in the next lesson.

# LESSON 21: IS OPTIMIZATION VALID?

## FORWARD ("BLIND") SIMULATION

A forward (or blind) simulation involves testing a system on one set of data, optimizing it, and then using the optimized parameter sets to test another set of data. The system is then evaluated based on the results for this second set of data. This approach avoids hindsight because the selection of the optimized parameter sets is done before the system evaluation, in contrast to the often used, but theoretically unsound, practice of basing performance evaluation on optimized results.

Again, the basic premise of optimization is that the best parameters of the prior period should continue to be among the better performing parameters in the future. To evaluate this hypothesis, we constructed the following test:

A simple breakout system was tested for 12 parameters (N=20 to N=130) on a portfolio of 10 markets (the same markets used in the diversification illustration in Lesson 9).

The number of contracts traded in each market was adjusted to approximately equalize the dollar volatility among the different markets. For example, since the average daily dollar price change per contract in T-bonds was five times as large as that of corn, five times as many contracts were traded in corn as in T-bonds. The system was initially tested for the 1984-1991 period, with parameters ranked based on their performance (measured by total profits) during that period.

The system was then tested for the subsequent 1992-1993 period, with the parameters ordered based on their 1984-1991 rankings. The parameter rankings in the 1992-1993 period were then compared with the corresponding rankings in the prior 1984-1991 period. If optimization worked, the parameters at the top of the list—that is, the parameters with the highest rankings in 1984-1991—should also exhibit high rankings in 1992-1993.

The same process was then repeated using the 1984-1993 period results to rank the parameters and then comparing those rankings with the rankings in the subsequent 1994-1995 period.

Finally, the process was repeated using the 1984-1995 period results to rank the parameters and then comparing those rankings with the rankings in the subsequent 1996-1997 period.

**Figure** 21-1 illustrates this process for a single market: cotton. The first column shows the ranking of the parameter during the prior period. The second column shows the ranking of the same parameter during the 1992-1993 period. Thus, for example, the first value listed in column 2 would be the 1992-1993 ranking of the parameter that ranked first in the prior period (in this case, 1984-1991). The second value listed in column 2 would be the 1992-1993 ranking of the parameter that ranked second in 1984-1991, and so on. Similarly, the first value listed in column 3 would be the 1994-1995 rank of the parameter that ranked first in the prior 1984-1993 period, and the first value listed in column 4 would be the 1996-1997 rank of the parameter that ranked first in the prior 1984-1995 period.

If optimization worked perfectly, the rankings in columns 2-4 would also be ordered from 1 to 12—that is, the ranking of a parameter in any given period would correspond to the ranking of the same parameter in the prior period. Of course, even the most ardent proponent of optimization would not expect such perfect duplication to be even remotely approached. However, if optimization worked, the rankings of parameters near the top of each column (the parameters that did best in the prior period) should be relatively high. (Note that a high ranking corresponds to a low number). Analogously, the rankings of parameters near the bottom of each column (the parameters that did worst in the prior period) should be relatively low (high numbers).

Therefore, if optimization worked, we would expect the two highest ranking parameters in each period (1, and 2) to cluster near the top of each column (implying those parameters had also performed well in the prior period). Similarly, the two lowest ranking parameters in each period (11, and 12) should cluster near the bottom of each column (implying those parameters had also performed poorly in the prior period).

**Figure** 21-1 indeed reflects such a pattern. In all three test periods, the two highest ranking parameters (1 and 2) had also ranked higher than the two lowest ranking parameters (11 and 12) during the *prior* period. Moreover, in two of the periods (1992-1993 and 1996-1997), the two highest ranking parameters (1 and 2) had also ranked relatively high in the prior period. In fact, in 1992-1993 and 1996-1997, the top ranking parameter in the prior period ranked first and second, respectively, in the subsequent period. Thus, the results reflected by **Figure** 21-1 seem to imply that optimization—selecting the best performing parameters in the *past* as the system parameters to be traded in the *future*—does add significant value.

However, if we examine the data for another market, such as the D-mark, the results seem almost exactly the opposite (see **Figure** 21-2). In this case, the best performing market in two of the periods (1992-1993 and 1994-1195) had ranked near the bottom of the list in the prior period (11 and 12, respectively). In the same two periods, the two worst performing parameters had ranked relatively high in the prior period. Also in these same two periods, the two highest ranking parameters (1 and 2) had ranked lower than the two lowest ranking parameters (11 and 12) during the *prior* period.

Thus, if one were to make a judgement based on the results in this table, the conclusion would be that optimization doesn't work at all, and perhaps might even have a detrimental impact.

Finally, there are markets that exhibit patterns such as the one reflected in **Figure** 21-3 for the gold market. (Note: this example is not shown in the video.) In this case, the results are a real mixed bag. In the first period (1992-1993), the two highest ranking parameters were those parameters that actually ranked lowest during the prior period. In the second period, however, the two highest ranking parameters had also ranked relatively high in the prior period ($2^{nd}$ and $4^{th}$, respectively). In the third period (1996-1997), the two highest ranking parameters had ranked right in the middle of the pack in the prior period.

Therefore, **Figure** 21-1 implies that one should trade the parameters that did best in the past; **Figure** 21-2 implies that one should actually trade the parameters that did *worst* in the past; and **Figure** 21-3 implies that the relationship between past and future performance is random. Which of these contradictory outcomes are we to believe?

In **Figure** 21-4 we combine the results of all 10 markets for the first simulation period (1992-1993). This table orders the parameters in each market based on their rankings in the previous period (1984-91) and shows their rankings for the subsequent period (1992-1993). Using T-bonds (symbol: US) as an example, the top ranked parameter in 1984-1991 was the second ranked parameter in the subsequent 1992-1993 period, and the lowest ranked (12) parameter in 1984-1991 was the next-to-lowest ranked (11) parameter in the subsequent 1992-1993 period. **Figures** 21-5 and 21-6 are analogous for the second and third simulation periods: 1994-1995 and 1996-1997.

If optimization worked, we would expect the best performing parameters of the current period to also have been among the higher ranked parameters in the prior period, and the worst performing parameters of the current period to also have been among the lowest ranked parameters in the prior period. Or, equivalently, we would expect to see the "1s" and "2s" clustered near the top and the "11s" and "12s" near the bottom. Scanning **Figures** 21-4, 21-5, and 21-6, we see no such pattern. Although there are many "1s" and "2s" near the top of columns and many "11s" and "12s" near the bottom—the pattern we would expect to see if optimization worked—the reverse occurrence is just about as common.

**Figure** 21-7 shows the average rank of the *prior* period best performing parameters in each market for each of the three simulation periods. These average rankings are compared with the simulation period average rankings using the worst performing parameters in each market in the *prior* period. The average rank for each period, which by definition always equals 6.5, is shown for comparison purposes. If there were no relationship between past and future rankings, we would expect both parameter classifications—those parameters that ranked highest in the *prior* period and those that ranked lowest—to exhibit average rankings not significantly different from 6.5 during the simulation periods.

The last row in **Figure** 21-7 shows the average of these average rankings across all three simulation periods. The all-period average rank for the *prior* period best performing parameters was modestly better than the average rank value of 6.5. However, the degree of improvement was modest enough so it is probably not significant. Moreover, the all-period average rank for the *prior* period worst-performing parameters was approximately equivalent to the rank for the *prior* period best performing group. Thus, this table fails to reflect any evidence that *prior* period best performing parameters are more likely to witness above-average performance in a subsequent period.

**Figure** 21-8 compares the 1992-1993 market-by-market profit/loss for four classifications of parameters:
1. the actual best performing parameter set in the given period (1992-1993);
2. the best performing parameter in the *prior* period (1984-1991);
3. the worst-performing parameter in the *prior* period (1984-1991);
4. the average of all parameters in the given period (1992-1993).

Note that these profit/loss statistics are based on a volatility adjusted position size. Thus, a market that witnesses much larger average daily dollar price swings (e.g., T-bonds) than another market (e.g., corn) will trade proportionately fewer contracts. **Figures** 21-9 and 21-10 are analogous for the 1994-1995 and 1996-1997 periods.

The following are the two salient points implied by these profit/loss tables:
1. None of the parameter classifications—best in *prior* period, worst in *prior* period, or average in current period—came even remotely close to approaching the returns of the actual best performing parameter in each period. Although this is hardly surprising, it does serve to underline the key point that optimized results will greatly inflate the actual performance that could have been realized in a prior period without the benefit of hindsight.

2. The *prior* period best performing group outperformed the *prior* period worst-performing group and the average of all parameters in the given period in all three periods. Thus, these tables appear to provide the first evidence of a significant improvement provided by optimization.

Although **Figures** 21-8, 21-9, and 21-10 imply that optimization improves performance, the effect may not be as significant as it appears. To place the degree of improvement provided by optimization in perspective, **Figure** 21-11 plots the total return for each of the four parameter classifications for the three periods combined. As can be seen, optimization (best *prior* period) captures only a small portion of the performance difference between the average of all parameters, which could be approximated by random parameter selection, and the actual best performing parameters.

More importantly, a market-by-market breakdown (**Figure** 21-12) shows that the superior performance of the *prior* period best performing parameters was primarily due to the Japanese yen (JY) and cotton (CT), and to a more minor extent gold (GC). In the 7 other markets, the *prior* period best performing parameters witnessed returns roughly equivalent or worse than the *prior* period worst-performing parameters or the average of all parameters. In fact, if we compare total profits for the three periods combined for the different parameter classifications excluding only one market—the Japanese yen—there is very little difference between the three groups (see **Figure** 21-13). Note also that the actual best parameter group (which cannot be determined until after the fact) outperformed the other three classifications by an approximate 3:1 ratio.

**Summary of Results:**

In terms of average rankings, optimization did not provide any improvement.
In terms of profit/loss, there was an improvement in all three periods.
However, this improvement was primarily due to 2 out of the 10 markets, rather than reflecting any consistent pattern, leaving open the question of whether it was a chance occurrence of the portfolio chosen. For example, if the portfolio didn't include the Japanese yen, there might not have been any evidence of the best *prior* period parameters doing better than the worst *prior* period parameters.

## CONCLUSIONS REGARDING OPTIMIZATION

- Any system can be made very profitable for the *past* with optimization.
- Remember, our system included only one parameter. Imagine the degree of improvement of past results that can be achieved by using optimization on a multi-parameter set system.
- If you find a system that cannot be made very profitable with optimization, congratulations because you have a found a system that can probably be traded very successfully in reverse.
- Optimization will *always* substantially overstate potential performance.

For most systems, optimization will improve *future* performance only marginally to moderately, if at all.

- The main usefulness of optimization is to define broad boundaries for parameter ranges.

- Fine-tuning optimization (e.g., testing a breakout system using parameter increments of 1 or 2 as opposed to 10) is at best a waste of time, and at worst self delusion.

- Complex optimization procedures are probably a waste of time. Simple procedures will most likely provide as much meaningful information.

Bill Eckhardt a very successful Commodity Trading Advisor and also, along with Richard Dennis, one of the trainers of a group of traders known in the industry as the "turtles" claims that human nature is so poorly attuned to trading that most people will get worse than random results. According to Eckhardt, the key human trait that interferes with trading success is the natural tendency for people to seek comfort. Seeking comfort will lead to trading decisions that feel good, but are usually wrong (for example, giving a losing trade just a little more time). As it pertains to trading systems, the trait of seeking comfort manifests itself in overoptimizing systems, which makes the system more comfortable to trade (because the past results look so good), but less likely to succeed in the future.

The foregoing is NOT intended to imply that optimization shouldn't be used to determine parameters to trade in the future, but rather to emphasize the following two principles:

> **CARDINAL RULE 6: Optimization should never be used to evaluate past performance.**
>
> **CARDINAL RULE 7: Never assume that optimization will meaningfully improve a system without rigorously testing the premise (e.g., blind simulation).**

In summary, the degree to which optimization is used to select parameters to trade will depend on the individual trader and the specific systems. The blind simulation approach can be used to gauge whether optimization adds any value in parameter selection.

## TESTING VERSUS FITTING

*Note: Although the optimization example we used in this lesson involved only a single parameter, most systems will contain multiple parameters; hence, the discussion in this section is phrased in the more general terms of parameter sets as opposed to parameters.*

Perhaps the most critical error made by novice users of trading systems is the assumption that the performance of the optimized parameter sets during the test period provides an approximation of the potential performance of those sets in the future. **Figure** 21-11 and **Figure** 21-13 dramatically illustrate the folly of using optimized results for system evaluation. As these charts demonstrate, the *prior* period best performing parameters, which is all we can determine without hindsight, will not even remotely approach the performance of the actual best parameters. Evaluating a system based on the optimized results (i.e., the results of the best performing sets during the survey period) can be best described as fitting the system to past results rather than testing the system. There are two reasonable approaches for evaluating performance:

**Blind Simulation Method**—In the blind simulation approach the system is optimized using data for a time period that deliberately excludes the most recent years. The performance of the system is then tested using the selected parameter sets for subsequent years. Ideally, this process should be repeated several times, stepping through time. The error of using hindsight in evaluating a system is avoided because the parameter sets used to measure performance in any given period are selected entirely on the basis of prior rather than concurrent data. In a sense, this testing approach mimics real life (i.e., one must decide which parameter sets to trade on the basis of past data). The optimization test detailed earlier in this lesson used this type of procedure, stepping through time in two-year intervals.

**Average Parameter Set Performance Method**—This approach assumes that performance is fairly represented by the average of all parameter sets tested. This approach is valid because you could always throw a dart to pick a parameter set from a list of parameter sets. If you throw enough darts, the net result will be the average. The important point is that the average should be calculated across all the parameter sets tested, not just those sets that prove profitable. Note that the trader might still choose to trade the optimized parameter sets for the future (instead of the randomly selected ones), but the evaluation of the system's performance should be based on the average of all parameter sets tested (which is equivalent to a random selection process).

The blind simulation approach probably comes closest to duplicating real-life trading circumstances. However, the average parameter set performance is probably as conservative an approach and has the advantage of requiring far less calculation. Both methods represent valid procedures for testing a system.

## THE TRUTH ABOUT SIMULATED RESULTS

Although the concepts discussed in this section are most pertinent to *buying* systems, most are also relevant to developing systems

"Simulated Results" could refer to three very different concepts:

1. **Real-time**—A system is designed and then signals are generated in real time, using realistic transaction assumptions. The results of such a rigorous approach would closely approximate the results of an actually traded account (if one existed). Consequently, this type of simulated results would have real significance.

2. **Minimal hindsight**—This description might apply to results derived by the *blind simulation* or *average parameter set* methods just described.

3. **Hindsight**—As the name implies, these simulated results incorporate past information. For example, if a breakout system is tested on a market, and a parameter value of 40 demonstrates the best performance, using this parameter value to represent the past performance of the system would be a hindsight simulation. Hindsight simulations area absolutely worthless in terms of evaluating systems.

There has been so much misuse of simulated results that I believe the situation is best summarized by what I call Schwager's corollary of simulations to Gresham's law of money. Gresham's proposition was that "bad money drives out good." Gresham's contention was that if two types of money were in circulation (e.g., gold and silver) at some arbitrarily defined ratio (e.g., 16:1), the bad money (i.e., the money overvalued at the fixed rate of exchange) would drive out the good. Thus, if gold were worth more than 16 ounces of silver, a 16:1 ratio would result in silver driving gold out of circulation (as people would tend to hoard it).

My corollary is: "bad simulations drive out good." The term "bad" means simulations derived based on highly tenuous assumptions, not bad in terms of indicated performance. On the contrary, truly "bad" simulations will show eye-popping results.

By using hindsight, it is easy to construct simulated results for a system showing returns of 100% per year, 200% per year, or more. Name any number you want. The point is that, given enough hindsight, it is possible to construct virtually any type of past performance results. The commonplace use of hindsight in simulated results for marketed trading systems means that if anyone tried to sell a system or a trading program based on truly realistic simulations, the results would appear laughably puny relative to the normal promotional fare. It is in this sense that I believe that bad (unrealistic) simulations drive out good (realistic) simulations.

How are simulated results distorted? There are a number of primary means. In reading the following list, keep in mind that many of these items pertain not only to marketed systems but also represent sources of performance result distortion that are pertinent to the system developer. These sources of distortion include:

**The Well-Chosen Example (Revisited)**—In constructing a well-chosen example, a system promoter might select the best market, in the best year, using the best parameter set. Assuming a system is tested on 25 markets for 15 years and uses 100 parameter set variations, there would be a total of 37,500 (25 x 15 x 100) one-year results. It would be difficult to construct a system in which at least one of these 37,500 possible outcomes did not show superlative results. For example, if you tossed a group of ten coins 37,500 times, don't you think you would get 10 out of 10 heads sometimes. Absolutely. In fact, you would get 10 out of 10 heads on the average of one out of 1,024 times.

**Kitchen Sink Approach**—By using hindsight to add parameters and create additional system rules that conveniently take care of past losing periods, it is possible to generate virtually any level of past performance.

**Ignoring Risk**—Advertised system results frequently calculate return as a percent of margin or as a percent of an unrealistically low multiple of margin. This one item alone can multiply the implied returns severalfold. Of course, the risk would increase commensurately, but many of the ads don't provide those details.

**Overlooking Losing Trades**—It is hardly uncommon for charts in system brochures or advertisements to indicate buy and sell signals at the points at which some specified rules were met, but fail to indicate other points on the same chart where the same conditions were met and the resulting trades were losers.

**Optimize, Optimize, Optimize**—Optimization (i.e., selecting the best performing parameter sets for the past) can tremendously magnify the past performance of a system. Virtually any system ever conceived by man would look great if the results were based on the best parameter set (i.e., the parameter set that had the best past performance) for each market. The more parameter sets tested, the wider the selection of past results, and the greater the potential simulated return.

**Unrealistic Transaction Costs**—Frequently, simulated results only include commissions but not slippage (the difference between the assumed entry level and the actual fill that would be realized by using a market or stop order). For systems that generate frequent trades, ignoring slippage can make a system that would wipe out an account in real life look like a money machine.

**Extracted Results**—This term refers to results that are based on actual trades, but that have been extracted from a larger group of trades. For example, assume someone develops a trading system and then uses the system signals to trade twenty markets. After five years, the total results are mediocre, but three of the markets have done exceptionally well. The system developer then decides to revise the program to trade only these three markets—nothing wrong with that—and then markets the system based on only the results of these markets—an action that is highly misleading *even though it based on actual trades*. Why? Because the selection of markets incorporates hindsight. It is one thing to decide to revise the market portfolio to be traded in the future based on past information and quite another to revise past performance results based on past information. *Therefore, even actual trading results are only meaningful if they represent the portfolio that was actually traded in the past, not a hindsight selected portfolio.*

As proof of the biased nature of advertised simulated results, I can assure you that you will never see any simulated results for a system that shows the system long the S&P as of the close of October 16, 1987. Advertised simulated results are very much like restaurant reviews written by the proprietors—you would hardly expect to ever see a bad review.

# LESSON 22: MEASURING TRADING PERFORMANCE

## EQUITY BASED VERSUS TRADE BASED PERFORMANCE MEASURES

Trade based performance measures are the type contained in the TradeStation performance table (see **Figure** 22-1). Trade based performance measures are OK for single market analysis, but for multimarket portfolios, equity based performance measures are more appropriate because we are concerned about answering questions such as:

What is the return on the capital allocated to the system across the markets traded? (Note capital allocated should not be confused with margin requirements, which would imply excessive leverage.)
What are the maximum and average drawdowns trading all the markets combined?

Both the funds needed to trade a system on a multimarket portfolio and the risk levels on the entire portfolio depend on the interaction of markets. Therefore, it makes much more sense to combine the individual market results into a single equity series. Equity based performance measures are also much more the standard—for example, all money manager or fund statistics are always equity based, not trade based.

## CALCULATING EQUITY-BASED RETURNS AND DRAWDOWNS FOR A PORTFOLIO—FUTURES CASE: CONSTANT ACCOUNT SIZE

### Form Equity Series

Define the markets traded and the number of contracts in each market. The position size for each market can be static (constant throughout the test period) or dynamic (e.g., adjusted by margin, contract value, volatility).

Test the system on the markets and the position sizes assumed in the preceding step.

Add the daily (monthly) profit/loss for each market to get a daily equity series (monthly).

Calculate Monthly Percent Returns.

Define the account size—a preliminary guess is fine.

If subsequent steps show that the risk implied by the assumed account size is too high or low, adjust the account size. (Note: The methodology for determining the account size appropriate to the individual trader will be discussed in greater detail in the next lesson.)

If a change in the account size is not desired (for example, if the implied risk indicates the need for a larger account size, but the trader does not want to allocate more funds), the alternative is to go back to step 1 in the Form Equity Series sequence of steps and redefine the markets traded and/or contracts traded.

Monthly percent returns are derived by the following formula:

Monthly Percent Returns =
Net Monthly Profit/Loss ÷ Constant Account Size

Longer term returns are equal to the sum of monthly returns because the account size is assumed to be constant

**Calculate Percent Drawdown**

Drawdowns can be calculated using the following formula:

Drawdown = (High Equity-Low Equity) ÷ Constant Account Size

*Note: The foregoing calculations are based on a constant account size. This constant account size could imply either literal monthly additions/ withdrawals or simply an understanding on the trader's part that the potential and risk are equivalent to the levels that would be realized trading the assumed constant account size.*

The constant account size will still be representative for the case when trading size is increased sporadically as funds permit. For example, assume the starting account level equals $100,000 and four years later $100,000 of profits have been accumulated and all position sizes are doubled. In effect, in this case, we go from a $100,000 account to a $200,000 account. Percent returns will remain the same as the constant account, since both returns and account size doubled.

## CALCULATING EQUITY-BASED RETURNS AND DRAWDOWNS FOR A PORTFOLIO—FUTURES CASE: VARIABLE ACCOUNT SIZE

The basic assumption of this approach is that *existing positions* and *trading size* are adjusted at the start of each month pro rata to the change in equity in the preceding month. Obviously such adjustments will only be possible for very large accounts, because it is not possible to trade fractional contracts. Nevertheless, this is the approach most relevant to measuring the performance of a fund or any large account. Monthly percent returns will be the same as the monthly percent returns of the constant account size. The equity series, however, will be different because of compounding. The following example compares constant and variable account size calculations.

**Example Assumptions:**

- $1,000,000 starting account size
- First month return = 10%; second month = 5%

**Constant Account Size Returns**

- First month: $100,000
- Second month: $50,000

**Variable Account Size Returns**

Account size varies with profits/losses and trading size adjusted proportionately.

- First month: $100,000
- Second month: $55,000 (5% of $1,100,000)

**Converting Monthly Return to NAV Series: Constant Account Size**
*(Note: This case not covered on the videotapes)*

- Starting Value: 1,000
- First month: 1,000 x (1+ (.10)) = 1,100
- Second month: 1,000 x (1 + (.10 + .05)) = 1,150

**Converting Monthly Return to NAV Series: Variable Account Size**

- Starting Value: 1,000
- First month: 1,000 x 1.10 = 1,100
- Second month: 1,000 x 1.10 x 1.05 = 1,155

**NAV Series Equivalent to Equity Series: NAV = 1,000 + (Equity Series/1,000)**

*Note: Although the video seems to imply that equivalence between equity series and NAV series applies only to constant account size, equivalence applies to variable account size case as well.*

**Constant Account Size**

|  | Equity Series | NAV Series |
|---|---|---|
| Starting Value | 0 | 1,000 |
| First month | $100,000 | 1,100 |
| Second month | $150,000 | 1,150 |

1. **Variable Account Size**

*(Note: This case not covered on the videotapes)*

|  | Equity Series | NAV Series |
|---|---|---|
| Starting Value | 0 | 1,000 |
| First month | $100,000 | 1,100 |
| Second month | $155,000 | 1,155 |

*Note: In either case—constant or variable account size—the equity series and NAV series graphs will appear identical if the NAV scale is selected to meet the following two conditions:*

1. *Minimum scale value of NAV chart is equal to 1,000 + (minimum scale value of equity chart/1,000)—for example, if minimum scale value of equity chart is -50,000, then minimum scale value of NAV chart = 1,000 +(-50,000/1,000) = 950.*
2. *Maximum scale value of NAV chart is equal to 1,000 + (maximum scale value of equity chart/1,000)—for example, if maximum scale value of equity chart is 1,000,000, then minimum scale value of NAV chart = 1,000 +(1,000,000/1,000) = 2,000.*

## CALCULATING EQUITY-BASED RETURNS AND DRAWDOWNS FOR A PORTFOLIO—STOCK MARKET CASE (LONG/NEUTRAL ONLY)

The stock market case is much more complex, and there is no single right approach for calculating equity-based returns and drawdowns for a portfolio. The following sections present two approaches that are far simpler than other alternatives—each of these approaches depends on a critical simplifying assumption.

**Method 1**—All Prevailing Positions Implemented at Start of Trading & Monthly Rebalancing

Run trading system for each stock in portfolio, using 1 share as the trade size.

Calculate percent return for each stock in each month. (Example: system long; stock price closes prior month at $10 and current month at $12; the percent return is 20%)

Based on the *simplifying assumption that the portfolio is rebalanced each month* (i.e., the total dollar investment in each stock is equalized at the end of each month), the portfolio return for each month is the average of the individual stock percent returns for that month.

Example (2-stock portfolio):
Stock A = 20% and Stock B = -10%
Portfolio return = (20%-10%) ÷ 2 = 5%

Use these monthly portfolio returns to create an NAV series, as was illustrated in the futures case. The NAV series can then be used to calculate percent drawdowns.

Although rebalancing may not be practical for all but very large accounts, this approach provides a consistent, reasonable method for representing performance. Also, even if monthly rebalancing is impractical, one can use annual rebalancing, which would mitigate the difference between actual trading results and the model. In any case, even if rebalancing is not used in actual trading, rebalanced simulations can still be used to compare different systems based on the reasonable assumption that the two methods (rebalancing and no rebalancing) will yield highly correlated performance rankings of different systems. In other words, if a system has superior performance with rebalancing, it will usually have superior performance without rebalancing. Therefore, rebalanced simulations can still be used to test and select systems even if rebalancing is not used in actual trading.

A second approach for calculating equity-based returns and drawdowns for a portfolio in the stock market case is presented in the following section:

**Method 2**—Only New Signals Taken (the simplifying assumption)

Example: Portfolio consists of 10 stocks each with $10,000 allocation

Run trading system for each stock in portfolio, buying $10,000 worth of stocks on every trading signal.

Portfolio account size is assumed to be $100,000. Reason: If signals were received on all stocks, the cash outlay would be $100,000 (even if the account size on later dates is significantly greater because of appreciation).

Add equity series of all individual stocks to get portfolio equity series.

Percent returns and drawdowns

= Change in portfolio equity ÷ $100,000

*Important Notes:*

*Until a new signal is received for every stock with an open (i.e., long) position at start of simulation, returns will differ from returns for same period indicated by simulations with earlier start dates. As an example, assume simulation with a starting date of 1/1/82 gets a signal for Stock X in 1982, buying at $10 and selling at $50 on 6/15/84. Simulations beginning in 1983 and 1984 would NOT show those returns—again because of simplifying assumption that only new signals taken. Thus, simulations with different start dates will yield different returns for the same year—the first year of the latter simulation and possibly the first few years.*

*If all open positions are implemented at the start of trading, then drawdowns measured from any start date would equal the drawdown between that day's equity and the subsequent low in equity. However, if only new signals are taken, a trader would not realize any drawdown due to existing open positions at the start of trading. Therefore, since this method assumes that only new signals are taken, it probably makes more sense to measure drawdowns from any point based only on trades entered after that point. Measured this way, the drawdown calculation for any given day would reflect the drawdown (if any) experienced by a trader that began using the system on that day. In this way, a drawdown could be calculated for every day (month) in the data series, based only on trades entered after that day (month).*

## THE NEED TO NORMALIZE GAIN

Consider the systems in **Figure** 22-2. Which would you rather trade? If profit was the only performance measure considered, you would come to the conclusion that System A is better. However, it should be obvious that almost all traders would actually prefer System B. The problem is that risk must also be incorporated in the evaluation.

System B is better for all the following reasons:
- System B's marginally lower return is far outweighed by its drastically lower risk.
- If one starts to trade System A at the wrong time—which is easy to do—the trader could experience *far lower returns* than System B and possibly even a net loss.
- Many traders will *abandon* System A midstream and hence never realize its higher returns and very possibly even experience a net loss.

- System B can be traded at greater leverage, because of its lower risk. Doing so could provide a higher net return at a lower risk.

Clearly return by itself can be a meaningless number—it needs to be normalized by a risk measure.

## RETURN/RISK RATIOS

### Sharpe Ratio

The standard form of the Sharpe ratio is given by the following formula:

$$Sharpe\ ratio = \frac{E - I}{sd}, where$$

$E$ = expected return (average monthly return)

$I$ = risk-free interest rate (The-bill rate)

$sd$ = standard deviation

The standard deviation is a statistic that measures the degree of dispersion in the data. (The standard deviation can be found in any spreadsheet or statistical software program.) Thus if monthly returns are clustered in a relatively small range, the standard deviation will be low, which will push up the Sharpe ratio. Conversely, if monthly returns are widely scattered, the standard deviation will be high, which will push down the Sharpe ratio. It should be noted that the above formula is for the monthly Sharpe ratio. To annualize the Sharpe ratio, multiply the monthly data figure by the square root of 12

The modified form of the Sharpe ratio is given by the following formula

$$Modified\ Sharpe\ ratio = \frac{E}{sd}$$

The modified form has the advantage of simplification (avoids need to incorporate T-bill rates in calculation). Theoretically, it is also more appropriate for futures systems for two reasons:

1. Futures traders still earn interest income on almost all funds.
2. The modified form will not be affected by leverage, whereas the standard form will. Thus, for example, doubling all the position sizes on trade signals (for the same assumed account size), which will double returns and double drawdowns, will not alter the modified Sharpe ratio, but will change the value of the Sharpe ratio.

There are two problems with the Sharpe ratio:
1. The risk measure of the Sharpe ratio (the standard deviation of returns) does not distinguish between upside and downside excursions. Thus, the Sharpe ratio would penalize a system that witnessed sporadic sharp *increases* in equity, even if the equity retracements were small.
2. The Sharpe ratio does not distinguish between intermittent and consecutive losses, because the risk measure of the Sharpe ratio (the standard deviation of returns) is independent of the order of the data points. For example, **Figure** 22-3 depicts two hypothetical systems, both of which experience 12 monthly returns of $4,000 and 12 monthly returns of -$2,000—but not in same order! Although both systems have the same return and System B would be deemed far riskier by virtually everyone, the two systems have the same Sharpe ratio.

**Return Retracement Ratio**

The Return Retracement Ratio uses a retracement measure to represent risk, which probably comes closer than the standard deviation to defining risk in a manner consistent with the way most traders actually perceive risk. The formula for the Return Retracement Ratio is:

$$Return\ Retracement\ Ratio = \frac{R}{AMR} \quad where,$$

R = average monthly return

AMR = average maximum retracement

The AMR is calculated in the following two-step process:
1. For each month, find the maximum drawdown that would have occurred if trading began in that month. (If the equity never went lower than that month, then the maximum drawdown for that month would equal 0.)
2. Average these monthly maximum drawdown figures.

Note that to clarify the exposition, we have used a simplified form of the Return Retracement Ratio, which is entirely sufficient for our purposes. The original formula for the Return Retracement Ratio (described in *Schwager on Futures: Technical Analysis* by Jack Schwager) uses a compounded return calculation in the numerator and a more complex calculation for the average maximum retracement.

## TRADE-BASED PERFORMANCE MEASURES

Thus far, this lesson has focused on equity-based performance measures. In this section, we review some key trade-based performance statistics:

**Total Net Profit**—Important, but should not be used alone because it doesn't reflect risk.

**Average Profit per Trade**—A low average profit indicates that the system is vulnerable to increases in transaction costs. For example, a system with an average profit per trade of $50 would be suspect no matter how favorable the other statistics. This statistic should only be used in conjunction with other performance measures because:

- It does not incorporate risk.
- It may unfairly penalize active systems—for example, a system that generated one trade with a net gain of $2,000 would rate better than a system that generated a 100 trades with an average profit of $1,000.

**Percent Profitable**—This statistic is not recommended as a performance measure because the amount of winnings relative to risk is far more important than how often you win. For example, a system that won only 30% of the time with an average profit per trade (all trades) of $2,000 would probably be far better than a system with a 70% win rate and only a $100 average profit per trade.

**Profit Factor**—This statistic is equal to the total profit of winning trades divided by the total loss of losing trades. Although the profit factor is possibly the best single trade-based measure, it should be used in conjunction with total net profits, because a system could have a high profit factor, but not make much money relative to other systems. For example, a system that over a 10-year period generated 9 winning trades of $200 and 1 losing trade of $100 would realize a paltry net profit of $1,700 and yet exhibit an astoundingly high profit factor of 18.

## TABULAR PERFORMANCE ANALYSIS

### Time Window Return Analysis

This table summarizes the best, worst, and average returns for a variety of time intervals (see **Figure** 22-4). This table provides a great deal of information in a very concise format.

### Drawdown Analysis

This table summarizes all the major drawdowns, detailing the following key statistics for each (see **Figure** 22-5):
- the maximum depth of the drawdown;
- the length of the drawdown, measured from the start until the low point;
- the length of the recovery, measured from the low point to a new high;
- the start and end dates of the drawdown.

## GRAPHIC EVALUATION OF PERFORMANCE

### Equity Curve

The equity curve shows the cumulative equity gain by a system. Here we assume that the equity curve reflects the results of trading the system for a constant account size—that is, the trading size is not adjusted for changes in equity due to monthly gains/losses. **Figure** 22-6 illustrates an equity curve for a system traded on an assumed $1 million account. (The reason for using a large account size in this illustration is that we will want to compare this chart to a chart that reflects adjustments in trading size based on monthly gains/losses. Such adjustments are only possible for larger account sizes, since it is not possible to trade fractional contracts.) The equity chart provides an excellent depiction of a system's performance, both in terms of gain and risk.

### Net Asset Value (NAV)

The NAV shows the growth of a $1,000 investment given the series of monthly returns realized by the system. The typical assumption is that trading leverage is adjusted to reflect monthly gains/losses. In other words, the standard assumption is that the NAV reflects compounding (although, as was shown earlier in this lesson, it is also possible to construct an NAV for a constant account size assumption). Thus, for example, if the starting account size is $1.0 million and the system makes 10% in the first month, the assumption is that the trading size will increase by 10% to $1.1 million for the second month. If the system then made 5% in the second month, this gain would be applied to the new account size of $1.1 million, not the starting account size of $1.0 million. The NAV at the end of the second month would be equal to 1,000 x 1.10 x 1.05 = 1,155.

**Figure** 22-7 illustrates the NAV chart for the same system depicted in the cumulative equity chart shown in **Figure** 22-6. **Figure** 22-8 compares the cumulative equity and NAV graphs, with cumulative equity show in dollars on the left scale and NAV shown on the right scale. Not surprisingly, the two graphs are quite similar. However, note that the NAV graph reflects a larger cumulative percent return, approximately doubling relative to the starting value, whereas the cumulative equity is well below the level that would imply a doubling in value (1,000,000). The larger percent gain reflected in the NAV graph is a consequence of the fact that the NAV reflects compounding, whereas the cumulative equity graph was drawn based on the assumption of a constant account size.

### Log scale NAV

Without getting into a technical discussion, suffice it to say that on a log scale chart equal percent changes will appear to be of equal magnitude. **Figure** 22-9 is a log scale version of **Figure** 22-7. Note that the spacing between equal intervals gets smaller and smaller as the values increase. This scaling compensates for the fact that nominal changes imply smaller percent changes as values get higher. Thus whereas a 100-point change is equivalent to a 10% change when the NAV is 1,000, the same point change is equivalent to only a 5% change when the NAV is 2,000. Note that on this chart, the two indicated drawdowns, which were approximately equal in percent terms, appear to be of approximately equal magnitude. In contrast, in **Figure** 22-10, which shows the same graph plotted on a conventional scale, the latter drawdown appears to be much larger (because it was greater measured in points), even though it was approximately equal in percent terms.

### Rolling N-month Return

The rolling n-month return shows the cumulative gain during the n-month period ending in each month. Typically n is set equal to 12. **Figure** 22-11 depicts a rolling12-month return. In effect, each bar depicts the prior 12-month return ending in the given month. Ideally, we want this chart to reflect not only good returns, but also relative stability in returns. The sample chart depicted reflects relatively good stability, with only one 12-month period showing a net loss.

### Underwater Curve Figure

The underwater chart shows the drawdown at each point measured relative to the prior peak (see **Figure** 22-12). Months in which there was no drawdown (i.e., new equity peaks) are marked by bars. The underwater sections of the curve (shaded areas) reflect periods when the system was below its prior peak. The deeper and wider the underwater areas, the greater the implied risk in the system.

## NEGATIVE RESULTS

Negative results are valuable as a catalyst for learning—both in regards to providing insights as to what went wrong, as well as an inspiration for future efforts. To quote the late novelist John Gardner: "In a perfect world, there would be no need for thought. We think because something goes wrong."

As a final comment, it should be pointed that the idea that a losing system can be transformed into a winning system by reversing the signals is a misconception. Typically, a significant portion of losses in a losing system, and sometimes all the losses, are due to transaction costs. If the signals are reversed, these transactions would still exist. Therefore, in most cases, a losing system will still be a losing or only a marginally winning system if the signals are reversed.

# LESSON 23: MONEY MANAGEMENT

## DETERMINING ACCOUNT SIZE

The account size should be selected so that it keeps worst drawdowns within tolerable levels. The following example illustrates the methodology for determining the appropriate account size for trading a system:

Assumptions:
Maximum Drawdown = 20% ($20,000)
Maximum tolerable risk level = 30%
Worst *future* drawdown = 2 x maximum drawdown

(2 x Maximum Drawdown) ÷ Account Size = Maximum Tolerable Risk

$$(2 \times \$20,000) \div A = 0.30$$

$$A = \$40,000 \div 0.30 = \$133,333$$

Rearranging the terms in the above formula, the account size can be determined by the following general formula:

Account Size = (2 x Maximum Drawdown) ÷ Maximum Tolerable Risk

If the second and average drawdowns are far below the maximum drawdown, then it might be justifiable to use a moderately lower multiple than 2. An underlying assumption is that minimal hindsight was used in developing the system. If this assumption is not valid, then the multiple of maximum drawdown would have to be larger. Also risk-averse traders should probably err in the direction of using a larger multiple

## METHODS OF CONTROLLING RISK

Make sure approach avoids open-ended losses, either implicitly in system rules or explicitly in exit rules.

Make sure trading methodology incorporates rules for handling sharp increase in risk (e.g., coffee goes from $1.00 and 200-point ranges to $2.50 and 1000-point average ranges).

Use margin/equity ratio as one indication of whether leverage is excessive

Make sure approach accounts for highly correlated markets in portfolio.

Adjust account size for changes in equity through time.

## METHODS OF REDUCING RISK

Diversify across uncorrelated markets.

Diversify into at least two systems. Note that two systems can always be traded for the same funds as one system. If the two systems were traded independently, the position size would be +2 when both were long, -2 when both were short, and 0 when the systems had opposite direction positions. By cutting these positions in half, the position size would be +1 when both system were long, -1 when both were short, and 0 when the systems had opposite direction positions.

Diversify into more than two systems if funds allow.

In choosing systems to be traded in combination with other systems, lower correlation may be a more important characteristic than superior performance.

# LESSON 24: STEP-BY-STEP SUMMARY AND OBSERVATIONS

## CONSTRUCTING AND TESTING SYSTEMS: STEP-BY-STEP SUMMARY

Obtain data.

Define system concept.

Program rules to generate trades.

Select small subset of data to test system.

Generate signals for this subset for a single parameter set.

Generate charts with signals marked.

Check to see program is doing what is intended

Are there any errors?

Are there any oversights? Some examples of oversights include:

System fails to generate signal when intended.

System generates trade signal when no trade intended.

System rules create circumstance where no new trade signal can be generated.

Corrections should be based on making system adhere to intended concepts *without regard to profit/loss impact in sample run.*

After necessary corrections have been made, repeat Steps 6 & 7

Check if program corrections fixed prior incorrect or unintended signals.

Make sure changes do not have unintended effects.

Only after fully satisfied system working as intended proceed to following steps.

Define market portfolio, including contract allocations.

Define parameter set list for testing.

Evaluate performance by average parameter set or forward ("blind") simulation.

Compare results to generic system:

in terms of return/risk;

correlation to generic and other systems developed.

## MY OBSERVATIONS ABOUT TRADING SYSTEMS

In trend systems, the method used to identify trends may be the least important part of the system.

Complexity for its own sake is no virtue.

The two reasons why diversification is important, besides the well-publicized reason of reducing risk include:

ensuring that major moves are not missed

bad luck insurance

If funds are sufficient, diversification can be extended to systems as well as markets.

Generally speaking, the value of optimization is overstated.

Optimized results should never be used to *evaluate* a system's performance.

Two meaningful testing methods include: forward ("blind") simulation and average parameter set.

So-called simulated results are often optimized results.

Analysis of successful systems often reveals the presence of many markets with one or more years of very large profits, but no years with correspondingly large losses (profits left to run/losses cut).

A market should not be avoided because of increased volatility.

Negative results can provide important insights.

Trading results often reflect the market more than the system.

Use constant dollar trade size assumption in testing stocks.

Use continuous futures in testing futures.

Use only a small portion of the data base to develop and debug a system.

In checking a system for accuracy, make changes that are dictated by intended operation, not to improve profit of sample run.